The
Struggle

TO MIN & SIS HOBSON
YOU ARE BEAUTIFUL PEOPLE OF GOD. PLEASE KEEP ME IN
PRAYER AND I APPRECIATE YOUR SUPPORT.

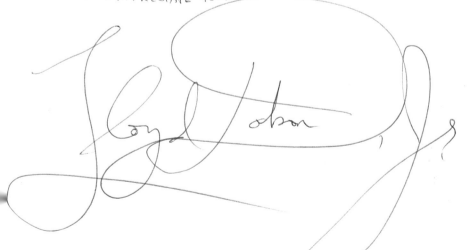

Lloyd Dotson, Jr.

The
Struggle

Lloyd Dotson, Jr.

PUBLISHED BY:
BRENTWOOD CHRISTIAN PRESS
4000 BEALLWOOD AVENUE
COLUMBUS, GEORGIA 31904

Acknowledgments

First and foremost I thank God the Father, Jesus Christ my Lord and Savior and the Holy Spirit for being my everything and for choosing an unqualified, unaccomplished author to show the world that it doesn't take credentials, but faith to do something that has been endorsed and blessed by God to do His Will. I thank my parents Mr. and Mrs. Lloyd and Shirley Dotson for their unending love, advice and support. Words fail me to properly tell you how much you mean to me. I love you both to life! Special thanks to my good friends Min. Leonard and Mrs. Patricia Kinsey for their love, prayers and support. Leonard I appreciate your diligence, honesty, perseverance and overall help in every facet of this project as your encouragement and prayers went a long way into making this become a reality. You are a friend that sticks closer than a brother, and I am honored that you heeded God's call by going on this journey with me as I embark upon the path He has placed me. I love you. My utmost gratitude and appreciation is extended to Mr. and Mrs. Eairrick and Suzette Kinsey for the blessing they shared with me. What God did through you was overwhelming and I will love you eternally for your kindness. Eairrick, thank you for letting me be your "second" little brother. My grandparents, who are no longer with me in the physical: Mr. and Mrs. Lewis and Eddie Lee Wiley. Pa-Pa instilled more in me the six years I shared with him before his death that no one else could have other than God Himself. To my grandmother, whom I affectionately called Mrs. Wiley. She commanded and demanded respect and taught me to do the same. The two of you will ALWAYS have a special place in my heart. Appreciation is shown to Mr. Jerry Luquire and Brentwood Publishing for allowing me to do this book without compromising what God directed me to do. Gratitude and appreciation is shown to Mr. Ken Grant for the awesome cover design that you created. You put into art what I envisioned in my mind and I couldn't say thank you enough for your skill and craftsmanship in doing so. I saved the very close second best thing to God in my life for last: my wife and children. Terry, thank you for putting up with me (as I do you ☺). I appreciate you for being my wife and the mother of my children. I wouldn't want anyone else to hold either position. I love you dearly. To Jeremiah, Jordan and Raven – go to bed! Just teasing (not really). Daddy loves each of you and I look for big things from you three as God uses you to His glory. Thank you for keeping me young. To you the reader, thank you for reading God's book. God bless you and I appreciate your support.

Foreword

Sunday, April 13, 2003. That would be the day that my life would change forever. Fortunately for me I had already come to know Jesus Christ as my Lord and Savior long before that. July 20, 1996 was the date I was married, so that milestone in my life had also passed. What is significant about this date is that on that date, I realized what God's destiny for my life was. We have dreams and aspirations in and of ourselves and ambition is all well and good. However, unless the Lord build the house, they that build it labor in vain. On this date, I realized who the builder not only was, but what it was the builder was going to build. It was on the aforementioned date that God laid out His blueprint for what my purpose was. I had known for quite some-time that God had given me the gift to write and that it was intended for the glory of God and to be used for His kingdom. However, I chose to do what most people do – nothing. But after what I would hear on this date, I could no longer do nothing.

As I sat in Sunday morning service listening to the minister pro-claim the Word of God, I enjoyed the message. Then, as part of his message, the speaker of the hour, Min. George Stewart, made the fol-lowing profound statement: "You spend 40 hours on your job, but do not spend 40 seconds on your gift and your gift is waiting to bust down doors for you." Upon hearing that statement, I can probably say that I don't remember another word he uttered. I was physically there and no I didn't fall asleep. I was merely captivated with the thought and the commanding resonance of what he had just said. God had spoken to me and let me know that I had books within me. Obviously, they weren't going to come out on their own. I didn't even make excuses about why I couldn't write them, I just didn't.

Later that evening, Min. Stewart's words continued to ring loudly through my mind, so loud that instead of trying to ignore them I did something different for a change – I went into action. I found myself on the internet seeking out information related to the process of publishing a book. My next step was to research pub-lishers to determine their method of accepting manuscript proposals. I continued to do all that I could think that was required. The more I looked, the more I found was needed. After having found about 70% of what is needed to publish a book I suddenly realized something – I didn't have anything to write about. I previously stated that unless the Lord build the house, they that build it do so in vain. That being said I had to wait.

Friday, April 18, my family and I were going to see a family friend in a play. My lovely wife had forgotten the directions, so we had to stop at a gas station to ask someone where to go. Upon getting the directions and going back to the car, God decided to give me some direction that man could never have provided – He gave me my first book. "Write a book and call it 'The Struggle'" is what He said. I got back into the car and my wife asked did I have the directions and I replied, yes but God just told me to write a book. She got behind the wheel as I patiently waited to hear God tell me more. He would give me bits and pieces of information, so much so, that I was forced to take a notebook and pen into the play with me so that I wouldn't miss out or forget anything that He wanted to let me know.

I began to type what God gave to me. There were times when He flowed through me like Niagara Falls and there were times when He made me feel dried up like the brook Cherith did the prophet Elijah. Nevertheless, God is faithful and He is not a man that He should lie. When He was ready, He gave me the words to put on the page. Had I forced the issue, this work would have been far below God's expectation and not accomplished what He intended. But because I stepped back and didn't interfere while the Lord built it, it has a foundation that is sure.

My prayer is that you will find this book to be a blessing to your life as a whole and your Christian walk in particular. Help spread the gospel of Jesus Christ by telling others about a glorified typist that is just trying to do God's will. While I am listed as the author, as men are attributed the authorship of books in the Bible, I know who deserves all glory, honor and praise. As such, give thanks to God for blessing us with His infinite wisdom and love by letting us know that even though we may have struggles in our lives, we have already overcome through Jesus Christ.

Contents

Chapter 1

Trapped

Another day, another dollar. Sam Banks got up with the same outlook on life as he did everyday – without much hope. As he put on his running shoes for his morning jog, he thought to himself how he really didn't want to do anything, much less go to work. "Might as well go run. At least I'll be in shape." Off he went as was his routine to run four miles each morning. Barely halfway into his workout, he felt raindrops. "The weather report didn't mention rain. Goes to show you how much they know." Sam turned back to get home before getting caught in the rain, but a downpour caught him before he could get to the end of the block. "Great, now on top of everything else, I'll have a cold to worry about" he thought. After making it back home, Sam got undressed and showered. Looking in his closet to find something to wear, he remembered his umbrella was in his car. "Now I'll get wet going to the car as well. Nothing seems to be going right this morning."

Sam arrived at his engineering firm at exactly 9:15. "They're waiting for you Mr. Banks" said his secretary. "Who, Sheila?" "The marketing group is meeting in Conference Room 3, did you forget?" "I totally forgot, how long have they been in there?" "Since about 9:00. You'd better hurry." Sam sheepishly entered the room trying not to be noticed. His supervisor immediately saw him and he knew a confrontation awaited. After the meeting adjourned, Sam's supervisor came over to ask why he was late. He offered a lame excuse and apology and quickly walked away from him. "This day was doomed from the beginning" thought Sam. He then went to get a cup of coffee which he proceeded to spill over his latest drawings. "I should have stayed in bed. This is the worst day of my life!"

The day ended and Sam couldn't have been happier to leave work. He left his office without shutting his computer down or putting away any of his equipment as he was accustomed to doing. "I'm getting out of here. Thank goodness it's the week-end." Sam came home from the office and was greeted by bill after bill. Seeing this made him more frustrated than he already was. Reluctantly, he began to check his voice mail. The first message was from his best friend Tim: "What's up dog! Do you live in the office or what? I was wondering if you ever decide to have a life if we could hang out tonight. Give me a call when you get in. Peace." Not really wanting to do anything but sit home and mope, he picked up the phone and gave Tim a call. "What's up Tim?" "Not much going on in my world, what about you?" "Same ol', same ol' with me dog? Where's the party at tonight?" "I heard about this club from a co-worker that is supposed to be the spot. Fine women and the whole nine yards. You down?" "Give me an hour and I'll pick you up."

Upon arriving at Tim's house, Sam suddenly had a change of heart. "I really don't want to go, but I'm already here now. Why didn't I feel like this in my driveway before driving all the way over here. Might as well go through with it." Tim heard the car drive up and bounded out of the door before Sam could get up the walkway. "Let's go man, no time to waste!"

"When are we going to get there?" asked Sam as it seemingly took forever to find the club. "Just be patient. Good things come to those who wait" replied Tim. "See, it's right there, where the crowd is gathered." After parking the car, the two went to stand in the night air as a line extended half a block outside the main entrance. There were going to be some of the hottest rap acts in the business performing and it appeared that everyone who was going to a club tonight was at this club. "Man we ain't going to ever get in! This line is too long. I know I should have stayed at home" remarked Sam. "Don't start complaining, we're already here" answered Tim. "Besides, what would you be doing if you were at home–nothing. I guess you're right. I'll make the best of it."

After an hour in line, they were finally inside. Tim's co-worker was right about this being a happening spot. The music was pumping, women were all over the place and the guys were doing their best to make their acquaintance. Not long after buying drinks, Tim noticed a young lady that caught his eye. "Sam, I'll be back. I'm going over there to meet that honey in the red." "Whatever. I'll be right here." Now Sam really didn't want to be here. He was frustrated from work, had nothing but bills at home to keep him company and now he had forced himself to go to a hot, crowded club that he really didn't want to be in. To make matters worse, his buddy had deserted him for the first woman he saw. In spite of the crowd, Sam felt so alone.

An hour passed by, then another. Sam not really enjoying himself just kept buying drinks. By this time, Tim had gotten to know the young lady he approached and they were dancing and drinking the night away. Sam decided that he had had enough and it was time to go. One thing however, he was drunk after hours of drinking. He pushed through the crowd to find Tim and let him know he was ready to go. Seeing as how Tim and this young lady were having the time of their life, they were not about to leave anytime soon. "Go on dog, I'll get with you later" Tim replied. So off Sam went. He knew he had no business driving, but reasoned with himself. I've done it before, I'll be okay.

Shortly after leaving the club, as he weaved his way home, Sam's worst fear came to pass – blue lights in his rear view mirror. "I knew I should have stayed at home. Where did he come from?" Sam slowly pulled to a stop and began to panic as he knew the smell of alcohol was strong on his breath. "What will I do. I know he's gonna bust me." "Too late to worry about that now, just have to deal with it." The officer slowly approached the car. Once he arrived, Sam stuck his head out of the window and asked "Is there a problem officer?" "Well, you were driving erratically. License and registration please." Sam reached for his wallet and insurance card. "I know I'm dead as soon as he smells my breath" Sam thought. The officer took Sam's information and went back to his cruiser to run a check. As the minutes passed, Sam anxiously waited for the officer to come back bearing bad news and to arrest him. To his surprise the next thing he heard was: "Drive a bit more carefully from now on." As he gave him back his license and insurance card, Sam breathed a heavy sigh of relief. "How in the world did I get out of that one?" Little did he know his escape was to be short lived. As he left his minor victory his mind began to wander and he lost his focus. Next he saw two bright lights and they were headed directly for him. Before he could swerve out of the way, he crashed into a pickup truck.

Dazed and groggy, he slowly began to open his eyes. "What in the world did I just hit?" "Felt like a brick wall." His mind said move, but his body didn't respond. After what seemed like hours passing by, he suddenly heard a voice: "Are you alright in there?" "Yes, but I'm trapped" Sam replied. "Hang tight, we're gonna get you out of there." But before he could follow through on his promise, Sam blacked out.

Chapter 2

What's Going On

"Where am I?" thought Sam to himself as he emerged from his sleep. "What happened, to me? Man does my head hurt!" "Good morning Mr. Banks." "Where am I?" Sam asked the person talking to him. It was a nurse at the hospital to which he had been taken. "You're in the hospital Mr. Banks. We weren't sure you were going to make it at first, but you pulled through." "Make it, make it from what?" "The accident. You don't remember it do you?" "No I don't. What happened to me." "Well, from what I understand you were driving home and you had a collision with a pickup truck." "What about the person driving the pickup truck?" Sam asked. "He wasn't as lucky as you." "You mean, he's…" "I'm afraid so" replied the nurse. "I'd better go and get the doctor to tell him you're awake. Take it easy, I'll be right back." "No, wait. This can't be happening. This is some sort of weird dream, worse yet a nightmare. I didn't kill anyone." "Calm down Mr. Banks, everything is going to be alright. The doctor will be right in."

Sam was overcome with emotions. "I didn't kill anyone. That can't be right. This isn't happening." But as he began to assess things, he realized the gravity of his situation. He looked down to see both legs in casts. His left arm was heavily bandaged and his head throbbed terribly. "This isn't a dream. I've been in a terrible accident and someone has died as a result. What was I thinking getting behind the wheel of my car after drinking so much. Now look what I've done." Just as he was having his pity party, the doctor came in. "Mr. Banks, I'm your doctor, Dr. Thompson. We weren't sure you'd make it. How are you feeling?" "Terrible, but not so much from the pain, I heard that the person I hit didn't make it." "Unfortunately that is the case. But let's concentrate on getting you better. You have some severe injuries but I can tell you are a fighter. Just get some rest and I'll tell the nurse what medication to give you for the pain." "Get some rest? Get some rest? I just found out I killed somebody and he's telling me to get some rest. I just don't see how." At that moment, Sam heard a voice say "You can find rest in me." "Who said that?" asked Sam. "It's me." "Me, who?" replied Sam. "God. You said you didn't see how you could get rest. I'm here to show you how. Rest in me Sam and you'll find rest like you've never experienced before." "How do I know this is God and not the painkillers talking to me?" Sam sarcastically replied. "When you drink do you hear anything as pleasant as what you hear now?" "No." "When you were given the drugs did you feel better for a moment and eventually need more to relieve the pain?" "Yes." "When you rest in me, you will never tire again. Also, I have pain medicine that will never require a prescription refill. Who else can make you that kind of guarantee Sam." At that moment, Sam was really confused, should he call the nurse or continue to listen. Although he liked what he heard, how could he be sure that he wasn't still drunk or worse yet hallucinating from all of the pain medication he was taking. He had never been a "religious" person. Sure he had gone to church a few times, but he was basically into doing his own thing his own way – without God anywhere in the picture. So why all of a sudden would God talk to him now? In spite of his uncertainty, he kept listening as God spoke to him.

"Sam, I'm here to offer you peace and rest, but it's just that an offer. I can't nor will I force you to accept. I heard you ask for rest so I came to give you rest. It's up to you Sam." "I just don't know" said Sam. "How can I be sure this is God talking. I've never heard Him before so how do I know what He sounds like?" "You must have faith Sam. You must have faith." *"Blessed are they that have not seen, and yet have believed.*'" After reasoning within himself, Sam drifted off to sleep.

The next morning, Sam woke up in excruciating pain. He rang for the nurse. "Yes Mr. Banks, how can I help you?" "I...I need some medicine. I'm hur-ting...hurting bad." "I'll be right there Mr. Banks." "The pain hasn't been this bad since I got here. What's going on now?" he thought. The nurse came in immediately. She began to adjust the flow of his IV to increase the medicine output. "You should feel some relief in a few moments Mr. Banks." "Thank you, I'm beginning to feel better already." "Glad I could help Mr. Banks." As the nurse left, Sam began to think about the conversation he had when God said that even though he took the pain medication he eventually needed more for relief. "Could that have really been God talking to me or was I just overcome with pain? I don't know, but at least I feel better now." Then the voice he heard on yesterday spoke to him again: "I could make you feel better all the time Sam. If you just trust me, all your pain will go away." "God, is that you?" "Yes Sam. It's me." "Why are you talk-ing to me. I've never bothered to take the time to talk to you. And besides, don't you know that I was in an accident and I killed someone and that's how I landed here in the shape that I'm in." "Of course I do Sam. I know all things. I heard you ask for rest and I came to give you rest." "And just how will you give me rest?" smirked Sam. "If you believe in your heart that my Son Jesus died for your sins and that He rose again on the third day and accept Him as your Lord and Savior, you can find peace and rest Sam. You must also not put any other gods before me for I am the Lord God and I am a jealous God. And Sam, you must repent of your sins." Do you understand what I have spoken to you? "I understand everything but the repent part. What does that mean?" "Repent means to turn away Sam. You must turn away from your life of sin and turn to a Godly life which I will direct. No longer can you do things the way you are accustomed. If you are going to follow Me

15

you have to trust Me to lead and direct your way. You must believe that I won't lead you astray and I won't leave you alone. If you do these things Sam, you can have rest. Would you like the rest I speak of Sam?" "Yes God. I need rest. I'm tired of going on the way I've been going." "Accept my Son as your Lord and Savior and not only will you receive the rest of which I speak, you will receive a pardon for your sins and the gift of eternal life in paradise with Me as opposed to the sentence of death and hell which would await you if you choose not to accept my offer Sam." "I choose you God. I want all of those things you just told me about." "You've just made the best decision of your life. Now, I didn't make you any false promises Sam. It won't be easy. The devil will do all that he can to make you feel as if you made a mistake. That is why I said earlier you must trust Me to lead you and know that you won't be forsaken or left alone. When you feel in despair always know that I am with you even until the end of the earth Sam. You are my child and I am your heavenly Father and I love you." "How can I know that I've made the right decision? I mean, I've tried other things in life that seemed to be 'safe bets' and they've all turned out for the worst." Well Sam, you've tried things out on your own without my direction. Now that I will take the lead I'll never lead you wrong or to failure. You will have peace that surpasses all understanding when you choose to walk with me and follow after my ways. That is how you will know you made the right decision." "Okay God. I'll give this a try. Nothing else has seemed to work and look at the situation I'm in now." "Everything is going to be alright Sam. *Trust in me with all thine heart and acknowledge me in all your ways and I will direct your paths.*[2]"

Sam had made a decision that would change his life forever. If he followed through on his end of the bargain and trusted God at His Word, he would have to totally change his way of life from what he was used to doing. Whereas he was used to being "The Man" at everything, now he would be dependent upon God to map out his every move. Would he be up to the challenge, or would he just "give it a try" to see what would happen.

Chapter 3

Recovery

As the days turned into weeks, Sam's condition gradually improved to the point where he was to be sent to a rehabilitation facility. "Time to get you into rehab Mr. Banks. We've done all that we can do for you here." "Thank you so much for everything you've done Dr. Thompson. I really appreciate it." "That's what we're here for. Now you just take it one day at a time and get back on your feet." "I will doc. I will."

Day one of rehab was not what Sam expected. He was pushed and pulled from every direction with no mercy from the therapist it seemed. "No pain, no gain Mr. Banks. Got to hurt to get better." "I thought God said there would be no more pain. He sure did give me a bum steer." "Did I?" "Who was that? asked Sam." "Sam you know my voice by now. I never said there would be no more pain. I promised that I could offer you pain medicine that didn't require a refill. Don't you remember Sam?" "Well, I guess that is what you said." "I know that is what I said." "*I am not a man that I should lie nor the Son of Man that I should repent.*[3]" "I also promised that even in despair I would never leave you nor forsake you. I see that you are in pain so I am here for you Sam." "God, forgive me. You're right. You have done exactly what you said you would do. I am the one who is complaining and not trusting as you

17

told me to. You'll have to give me some time to get used to this, I'm new at it you know." "I know Sam. I'll be patient with you as I am with all of my children."

Day two brought more of the same. Push, pull, massage. Push, pull, massage. "When am I finally going to get the chance to walk?" "That will come in due time Mr. Banks. For now this is what we need to do to get you to that point. Your muscles have experienced a significant amount of trauma, not to mention you haven't used them in quite some time. We've got to get them stimulated before we shock them into being used again. Don't want to set you back before you go forward now do we?" "I guess you know what you're doing. I'll keep quiet and let you do your thing."

This routine continued for about two weeks. Sam grew more impatient. "Exactly how much massage and whirlpool therapy is necessary before I can walk? I feel like I've gone through enough of this for every accident victim in Atlanta!" "Well Mr. Banks you haven't had that much therapy. Just be patient. You are going to get the chance to walk. Just remember, it won't be easy when it comes." "I don't care, I just want to get out of this chair and onto my own two feet." You will Mr. Banks, you will."

Sam continued in therapy and fought through the pain to regain the use of his legs. Although it was quite intense and sometimes he felt like giving up, this time there was something different. When he was ready to give up there was something inside of him that kept him going. Something he couldn't explain and had never experienced before. Finally, the time came for him to begin the process of learning to walk again. "Mr. Banks, the time you've been waiting for is here. We are going to work on walking today!" "Great, I'm ready. Let's get going." Unlike the previous therapy which was done in his room, he was taken to a room filled with all sorts of machinery and apparatus to help one learn to walk again. "Is all of this stuff necessary to teach me how to walk again." "Well not all of it. We use the different equipment for different patients and situations. Some are more extensive than others and some less. In your case we are going to start you off with this." Sam was shown a walker and a carpeted floor area on which he was to walk. "This is for old folks. I don't need a walker. I run four miles everyday. Just get me out of this chair and you'll see." "Now, now Mr. Banks, you have to crawl before you walk. You can't come roaring out of the chair, rather one step at a time. You'll get to that point, but this is where we are going to start you off. Slowly acclimate yourself to walking so that you can regain the strength in your legs." "Whatever, give it here." As soon as Sam grabbed the handles on the walker, he realized just how weakened he had become. "Man, I'm not as strong as I thought I was." "I told you Mr. Banks, you've gone through quite a recovery and your body is still doing so. It's going to take some time but you're going to get there." Sam began the slow process of regaining the strength in his legs. He was frustrated, but determined.

After using the walker, Sam graduated to using crutches to balance himself while continuing to strengthen his legs. "That's it Mr. Banks. You're doing great!" "Thanks. It hurts, but I have to keep pushing." Sam showed remarkable recovery abilities. In two weeks he was at the point most patients don't arrive until after four weeks of therapy. He so impressed his therapist, that his schedule was accelerated to accommodate his rapid progress. "Mr. Banks, at the rate you're going, you'll be out of here in no time." "That's what I want to hear. I'm more than ready to get out of this place and go home. Seems like I've been here forever." "Just keep doing what you're doing and you will be home very soon."

Next up for Sam was giving up his crutches and walking on the treadmill. This was a moment of truth for it was the first time he would walk on his own without any assistance since the accident. "Today's a big day Mr. Banks. You're going to walk by yourself for the first time." "I'm ready. Been waiting for this day for quite some time now." "We're going to start you off slowly and gradually increase the speed so as not to do too much too fast." The therapist started the treadmill on the slowest setting. Sam saw this and argued that he could go faster. "Crank it up. I can handle it." "No Mr. Banks, I can't do that. You'll only be hurting yourself if I put it on a higher setting." "But this is too slow, I need to pick up the pace so I can get out of here." At that moment, the phone rang. "I'll be right back Mr. Banks. You're doing just fine." As the therapist left to answer the phone, Sam looked to see if anyone was paying attention. Then he seized the opportunity to turn up the speed. "Now, that's more like it. See, I can do this. That therapist doesn't know Sam Banks." All of a sudden, Sam's left leg began to stiffen and he couldn't maintain the speed of the treadmill. "What do I do now?" Sam thought. "I know, I'll turn it back down." Just as he reached for the controls, he fell down face first. The therapist heard the noise and ran to Sam's aid. "What happened Mr. Banks? Are you okay?" "I think so. It's just that I'm so anxious to get out of here I may have been too aggressive for my own good." "I'll go and get a doctor to make sure you didn't reinjure yourself."

The doctor hurried into the room and gave Sam a mini check-up. "Mr. Banks, you cheated serious injury. I know you are ready to get back home and on your feet but you have to be patient and do what the therapist tells you or else you're going to be back to square one." "Okay doc, I hear you." Sam sat and pondered his next move as he thought about what the doctor said. "They think they know everything, but they don't know Sam Banks." "But I do." "Is that you again God?" "Yes Sam, it's me. I see you haven't been seeking me." "What do you mean?" "*I am a rewarder of those that diligently seek after me.*[4] Sam, just because you heard my voice and chose to accept my Son as your Lord and Savior, doesn't mean that is all. You have to follow after Me by studying My Word. And it's not something you can do when you feel like it, it must be done daily." "Study your Word?" "Yes Sam, study My Word. That is how you will get to know My ways and My will for your life. You think you've gone through a difficult period in your life. Sam you are really going to need Me to make it through what you're about to face. I'm here, but as I said before I offer myself to you and I can't and I will not force myself upon you. The choice is yours to make Sam. It's up to you." "I hear you, but right now I'm just concentrating on walking so that I can get back home." "Sam I can help you do that and more. Once again, as I told you before you have to trust Me."

That night as Sam lie in bed unable to fall asleep, he remembered what God said to him: *"I am a rewarder of those that diligently seek after me.⁵"* Sam had read the Bible on occasion and the few times he had gone to church, but he never had made a habit of reading one on a daily basis. Matter of fact, he didn't even own a Bible. In his hospital room, there was a Bible in the drawer. He took it out and opened it up to the beginning and began to read Genesis. *"In the beginning God created the heaven and the earth.⁶"* Instead of giving it a chance, he didn't see the need to read any further. "Why do I need to know that God created the heaven and the earth? I'm here now aren't' I?" In response God said to Sam: "Yes you are Sam, but you need to know how you got here and where you started from. My Word is vital to every aspect of your life and everything in it is necessary for you to have victory in your life – from the beginning to the end." "Sam as I told you before, you must have faith. *I have given to every man the measure of faith.⁷* It is up to you to grow that faith and build it that you may benefit from the security only I can provide. Have faith in me Sam and stop trusting in your own abilities. Sam, trust in Me."

The next morning presented a new challenge as Sam was faced with getting on an exercise bike. "Come on Mr. Banks. We're going to attack this differently. Don't want to tempt you to hurt yourself by speeding up the treadmill. Instead, we're going to put you on the exercise bike for a workout." "Anything that will help me get closer to the door." "Alright, let's begin." Sam climbed onto the exercise bike. He pedaled slowly at first as the pain shot through his legs as he bent his knees and thrust down on the pedals. "This hurts more than the treadmill did." "I know Mr. Banks. You're working more muscles, but you asked for it didn't you?" "I guess so, but boy does it hurt!" "Remember what we said in the beginning, no pain, no gain." "You're right." So Sam continued to pedal. Eventually it got easier as he forced himself to push through the pain. Before he knew it an entire hour had passed. "Whew! I'm beat. How long did I go?" "An entire hour. That's remarkable Mr. Banks. I've had patients take weeks to get up to an hour." "You've never had a patient like Sam Banks before." "Can't say that I have Mr. Banks. Can't say that I have." With that, Sam gloated his way into the shower before getting ready for bed.

The days turned into weeks and before you knew it, Sam was able to walk again. He had worked hard to get to this day and finally it was here. The therapist said the magic words he had longed to hear: "Mr. Banks, you're going home today." "Yes, I'm outta here!" shouted Sam. He couldn't nor did he try to hide his excitement. But as was his narrow escape from the police officer quickly replaced with tragedy, so too would this moment in his life.

Chapter 4

Facing the Music

Tim arrived at the rehabilitation center early and waited as Sam's discharge paperwork was completed. Once all the I's were dotted and T's crossed, Sam came out of the door wearing a big smile. "What's up man! Glad to see you on your feet again." "You know you can't keep a good man down." They got in the car and began to drive off.

"I'm sorry I let you down man" said Tim softly. "We're friends and I shouldn't have let you drive like that." "While I appreciate the apology, I can't put that on you dog. I'm a grown man and I knew the consequences. Anyway, it's all behind me now. Just get me home." "Well, it's not exactly behind you. I don't know how to tell you this, but you were charged with vehicular homicide in the death of the other driver." "You know I completely forgot about that! I was so wrapped up in my own world and how messed up I was I didn't even consider that. What was the guy's name?" "His name was Carl Jenkins." "Did he have a family?" "I don't know all of that. I just know that the cops came poking around and they were waiting to see how you came out of this to know when and what to do about charging you. I found you an attorney. What I suggest you do is call him as soon as you get home and see what type of arrangements can be made to turn yourself in. Sorry man." "It's not your fault. How in the world am I going to make it through this."

Sam arrived home and found everything just like he left it. The pile of bills had grown, but other than that everything else was intact. He sat for a moment and thought about his fate and what awaited him. Hesitantly he picked up the phone and dialed the number of the attorney Tim had told him about. His name was Dan Turner. "Dan Turner attorney-at-law, may I help you?" "May I speak with Mr. Turner please?" "May I ask who's calling?" "Tell him it's Sam Banks, my friend Tim Parsons referred me." "Just a moment." A long pause seemed like forever as Sam held on the line for Mr. Turner. Then suddenly, "Dan Turner may I help you?" "Mr. Turner, I'm Sam Banks and my friend Tim Parsons referred me to you." "Yes sir, how are you?" "I'm fine." "He has briefed me on your situation. I assume you've been released from the hospital and therapy?" "Yes, I just got home." "Hope you're doing better." "I am physically, but I'm scared to death of what I'm facing legally." "Stay calm son. While you do face serious charges you do have a few things going for you. This is your first offense and we're going to do all we can to help you. Unfortunately, you do need to turn yourself into police custody to face these charges. I can arrange to do that so that you won't appear to be fleeing from justice. But you need to do this as soon as possible." "I understand. Let's go ahead and get it over with." "Alright, meet me at my office. Do you know the address?" "Yes, Tim gave it to me. I'll be right over."

Sam called himself a cab and nervously awaited its arrival. "What will they do with me? How much will my bail be, if I even get bail? I've never been so scared before in my life." "Sam, I'm here for you." "God is it you?" "Yes Sam, it's Me." "If you're here for me then get me out of this mess I'm in." "Sam, *whatsoever a man soweth, that shall he also reap.*[8] You are guilty of what you've been accused Sam, but that doesn't mean that I will leave you. I will be with you and I am here for you." "What good is it if you're here for me but you won't help me out of this jam?" "Sam if you go through this without me, you will see how bad off you will be. It is better for you to allow me to help you through this and not go it alone. As I said to you before, trust Me Sam." At that moment, the cab blew its horn. "Whatever, I guess you're going with me to turn myself in too, right God?" "Have faith Sam, you must have faith."

The ride to Mr. Turner's office was short. Once there Sam met Mr. Turner who told him what to expect once they arrived at the police station. He would be booked and fingerprinted, have his picture taken and be officially charged. After this, Mr. Turner said he would immediately ask for a bond hearing to get the matter before a judge. "How long do you think I'll be in jail Mr. Turner?" "I can't say Sam, but I'll do my best to make your stay as short as possible."

Once at the police station, everything happened just as Mr. Turner had indicated. Before being taken to his cell, Sam pleaded with Mr. Turner: "Get me outta here." "I'll do all I can son. Trust me." Now inside his cell, Sam sat and stared at the ceiling. "I don't want to be in this place. But Mr. Turner is gonna work things out. I know he will." "Oh really?" "Who said that?" "Sam this is God. I see you trust Mr. Turner." "Yes, he seems like he's on the up-and-up." "And just how do you know that Sam?" "I can tell." "You can tell." "Yes. He seems like he's the type of guy that will take care of business and work on getting me out of here. Besides, he told me to trust him." "Just as I told you to trust me." "Yes, but..." "Mr. Turner you just met and you put your trust in him, however, I am the Lord God Almighty and you fail to trust Me? How interesting. Sam I told you while you were in rehab that you were going to face a period in your life in which you would really need Me to help you through. You will always need Me, but you need Me now more than ever. Sam I continue to make Myself available and you continue to refuse My help and My love. Know this Sam: *I stand at the door and knock. If any will answer I will come in and sup with him.*" Sam was more confused than before. He wanted to trust Mr. Turner to get him out, but even though he didn't have an established relationship with God he knew that he would probably be better off trusting in Him. "What should I do?"

Sam went back and forth in his mind to the point where he developed a headache. Finally, he fell asleep.

The next morning Sam was aroused by the sound of the guards yelling in the hallways. "Open cellblock 4!" "Man, I don't want to be in this place" Sam thought to himself. "I sure hope Mr. Turner makes something happen today." A short time later, Sam was removed from his cell and taken to a large cafeteria. There, along with the others he was given breakfast: lukewarm oatmeal, rubbery bacon, toast, an apple and a carton of milk. "This is disgusting. Don't they have anything else. I can't eat this. But I don't have another choice now do I." As Sam began to eat breakfast he checked out his surroundings and the other inmates. There were some unsavory characters that he didn't like the look of. "Sure hope I don't have any trouble in here. I'll just lay low and watch my back." At that moment, someone came and sat directly across from him. "What's up man. What's your name?" the guy asked. "And just who are you?" smirked Sam. "My name is Philip, but you can call me Phil." "I'm Sam." "Recognized you as a new face, don't want any trouble just thought I'd come over to say what's up." "I appreciate that. How long have you been here?" "About a month. I'm awaiting my trial date." "What did you do?" "Tried to rob a gas station. Things had gotten pretty bad for me. I lost my job, then my wife left and I was on the verge of losing my house. Instead of waiting to see things through, this is what the result of my actions got me." "Man, you were dealing with a lot of stuff." "True, but that's still not an excuse. When all of this began to happen I took my eyes off God and began to focus on the things around me. Before you know it I thought it was me against the world and here I am." "Wait a minute, you 'took your eyes off God?'" "That's right. I took my eyes off God. Unfortunately, when all was going good in my life I didn't think I had much need or any need for that matter of God in my life. So I was going through the motions of acting like I had a relationship with Him while truly believing that I was responsible for all that I had. As I look back now I know that without Christ I had nothing. However, it's not too late. Even though I'm facing a prison term, knowing Him means that I won't be facing it alone." "Wait a minute, wait a minute. You mean to tell me that you still believe in God?" "Absolutely. More than I did before. When I first got here I thought that all hope was lost. But I read in His Word that '*I can do all things through Christ which strengtheneth me.*[10]' After reading that I prayed and asked God if I could apply that to my situation. He let me know that even though I was in a physical prison I could still be spiritually free. That's the approach I've taken ever since and intend to maintain."

Phil and Sam continued talking until breakfast was over. During the time they were allowed to be out of their cells they shared with one another situations that each one could relate to. It was as if two old friends were getting reacquainted. The day passed quickly and it was time for lockdown for the night. As they went to their respective cells Phil left Sam with this thought: "The Bible says '*Ask and it shall be given you, seek and ye shall find; knock, and it shall be opened unto you.*[11]' I urge you to do what that suggests."

Sam sat alone in his cell looking back over the day's events. Instead of trouble he found a friend. And not only that he received advice that seemed as if it would help him make it through. In spite of where he was, Sam now had a different perspective on things. "Instead of me moping around while I'm here, I'm going to make the best of things and get my life together" Sam declared.

Morning came and Sam was awakened by the sound of his cell door opening. "You've got a visitor." It was Mr. Turner. Sam was taken to a room where Mr. Turner was seated. Sam walked in and the two shook hands. "Got any news for me?" asked Sam. "Well Sam, I found out who the judge handling the case will be and we've got a tough one. He's not generally known to grant bail but that doesn't mean we're not going to try." "What are the odds Mr. Turner?" "I don't want to get your hopes up, nor do I want to deflate them. We'll just do our best to work on getting you out."

Sam was taken back to the recreation area where the inmates were allowed to workout, play cards, etc. He saw Phil with a group of guys. "What's going on?" "Nothing, just shooting the breeze." "Phil, can I talk to you for a minute?" "Yeah man, what's up?" "I just saw my lawyer and he said that I have a tough judge that usually doesn't grant bail." "While I understand your lawyer is giving you the point of view as man would see it, you've got to trust God. That's who has the final say so." "You've really been coming at me hard about God and trusting in Him." "Sam, don't you realize that's all we have to trust in. Whether you're incarcerated or not you still need Him. There is no way of getting around it. When you were going through life before were you miserable or happy?" "Miserable." "My point exactly. With Jesus Christ in your life, even in a place like this you can find joy. It sounds crazy, but it's possible. Remember what I told you last night about asking and it would be given to you and seeking and finding?" "Yeah." "Most people misinterpret that to mean material/tangible things. Those things are nice and we do need them. But God was telling us that the stuff money can't buy is what is most important and the only way we can get it is through His Son Jesus. If you don't have peace of mind but a million dollars in the bank, you'd go crazy trying to figure out how to spend it." "You've got a point there Phil." "But even when you're broke, with Christ you have peace because you know some way, some how, things are going to work out. That's what I forgot when I chose to rob that gas station. Regardless of my mistake however, Christ is still going to see me through. I have to pay for what I did because He doesn't overlook our sins. He forgives us of them and helps us not to repeat them. That's the difference in having Christ in your life as opposed to going it alone."

That night as Sam sat in his cell he thought about all the things that God had said to him during his hospitalization and rehab stint. The recurring theme was 'trust.' Now he sits in jail and the very first person he meets is Phil who is preaching the same message of trusting in God. While he was in the hospital he made the half-hearted decision to follow after God and accept Jesus as his Lord and Savior, he hadn't really committed his life and ways to Christ. But here it was being brought up again. "Why all of a sudden am I so special to God?" "What about when I was a kid and my dad walked out on my mother and two sisters and I. Or college when I struggled to make ends meet. Where was God then, huh?" "I was there for you then Sam just as I am now. You've always been special to me, and I've always been with you. Sam, you must understand that because of my grace and mercy even though the situations you encountered seemed like they would overwhelm you, they didn't. That's because *I the Lord am your keeper.*[12] Because I did keep you safe and protected you, you weren't swallowed up by the seas of misfortune. Rather you were able to persevere and overcome." "God I'm confused." "I'm here to help you my child." "Well, I'm going through life and thinking I'm getting by on my own, but you tell me that you've been keeping me." "That's right." "*When you were yet without strength, in due time Christ died for the ungodly.*[13] That means even when you thought you were doing it all on your own you weren't. My Son and His power keep you until you recognize that you need that power. Do you understand that Sam?" "I think so. While it appeared that I was doing my own thing, it was Jesus doing it for me?" "That's correct Sam. And unlike man who would require and demand payment for his services, all that I require is that you follow and trust Me to lead you. No strings attached."

Chapter 5

Change

An entire month passed by and Sam was still in jail. Mr. Turner had not been able to persuade the judge to grant a bond hearing. Not only that, the grand jury was about to consider his case to be bound over for trial. One morning after breakfast, Phil approached Sam. "Guess what. My lawyer got me a plea bargain." "Is that good or bad?" asked Sam. "Good for me. I was looking at 10 or more years for armed robbery. But I asked God for mercy and he showed me some. I was offered a plea bargain of five years plus five years probation with a maximum time to be served of three years." "Well if you say it's good news then I guess I'm happy for you man." "I know it won't be easy, but I am going to trust God to take care of everything. "When will you be transferred to the facility to begin your sentence?" "Sometime tomorrow. Since they worked this out so quickly, the paperwork should only take a day or so and I'll be leaving here. I'm glad I got a chance to meet you Sam. I'll be praying for you and I hope you will do likewise for me." "Yeah man, I will."

Now what was Sam to do. The one friend he had met was about to be transferred and he would be all alone again, or so he thought. Sam then remembered some of the conversations that he and Phil had had during the past month. One thing Phil always encouraged

Sam to do was to seek after God, whether by prayer or studying His Word. Would Sam have the desire to do this on his own or would he now go back to his old habits of doing things his own way.

Morning came and just as Phil had predicted, his paperwork was completed and he would be transferred after breakfast. "Well, unless something strange happens, we won't be seeing each other for a while" said Phil. "I just hate we had to be in jail to meet one another" said Sam. "Would have been much better on the outside." "True, but just the fact that we met is better than not having met. Remember what I told you: *God is a rewarder of them that diligently seek Him.*[14] Whether I'm here or not, you need God Sam. He is not going to force feed His Word down your throat. You have to desire to have Him on your own. Unfortunately being in here should make that a lot easier, because this is a place that can quickly take your sanity away. However, in God you can find peace in the midst of a storm, even in the midst of a prison cell. Take care Sam and remember God loves you." And just like that, Phil was gone.

Sam recalled Phil's words carefully that night. Not just the last things he said to him but everything they talked about over the past month. Now he would really be challenged to see if he had in fact been taking Phil's advice to heart or merely passing the time. He was sitting in jail with little or no hope for bail, his case was about to be bound over to the grand jury and who knows which way they would decide on disposing of his case. After going over all this, Sam got down on his knees and said this prayer: "God, I'm not accustomed to doing this, matter of fact I don't have any experience at praying. But Phil told me to just talk to you from my heart. I'm scared God and I don't know what else to do. You said I could trust you but it is hard to trust in someone I can't see. Anyway, I plan on giving it my best shot and hope you will see me through. Thank you for listening to me God."

Sam began to read the Bible. Not everyday, but considering that he never read before this was a good starting point. He saw a lot of interesting stories that he had heard about, but casually dismissed as fairy tales or fables passed down through the ages.

He read about David and Goliath, the story of Samson, etc. "These guys made mistakes just like me and they're mentioned in the Bible?" Sam questioned. "How could it be that people that have so much failure be mentioned in God's Word?" "Because I get the glory out of those types of situations." "God is that you?" "Yes Sam, it's me. I used the people you read about because if people had all of their ducks in a row then when you read My Word you would feel like you couldn't measure up to what I had chosen. The only perfect person I used to do anything on My behalf was My Son Jesus Christ. Other than Jesus, everyone else that I used in the past and use now has sinned for My Word declares that *All have sinned and fallen short of My glory.*[15] As a result there is no way for anyone to feel that they are better than anyone else. In spite of that Sam, they all had to have faith to do what I asked of them. *Whatsoever is not of faith is sin.*[16]"

Another day passed and Mr. Turner came to see Sam. "How are you holding up son?" "It's hard Mr. Turner. I want to get out of this place so bad. I know you do Sam. I'm here to tell you that the grand jury has bound your case over for trial. I'm pushing for a speedy trial that would place yours on the books within a matter of weeks instead of months." "Whatever you think is best Mr. Turner. I trust you to do the right thing." "I'll do my best for you Sam. You can count on that."

One evening, just as he was going to lift weights, a guard approached Sam. "You've got a visitor." Sam thought it was Mr. Turner with news of the upcoming trial, but to his surprise it was Tim. He hadn't seen Tim since he was released from rehab. "What's up man, what took you so long to come to see me?" "I couldn't bring myself to come before now. I know I should have but I just didn't want to see you caged up like some animal. You're my friend and I've been feeling so much guilt about what happened. How can I tell you how sorry I am." "We've been through this already Tim. I knew the consequences of what could happen driving drunk and I chose to take the risk. Now I have to pay the price. It's not your fault so stop beating yourself up. Besides, I met a guy named Phil who really gave me some helpful advice." "And just what was that?" "Well, he told me to trust in God." "Trust in God, man you're tripping. If God was all of that and could be trusted in to come through, why can't you get a bond hearing to get out until your trial?" "While I can't answer that I know since I've been doing what Phil suggested, I've been having a better go of it in here. Being in here can drive you insane, but I have had a calming effect come over me that I can't explain and I've never felt before." "Man, you've still got all those drugs in you from your rehab." "No, this isn't drugs. This is something totally different. There aren't words I can use to describe it really." "Man, I'm out of here you've gone crazy. That's why I didn't want to come up here." "Wait Tim, I'm not crazy, you need to hear me out." "I'll come back some other time man. Take care of yourself." Not wanting to hear another word, Tim abruptly got up and left the room. Sam was left to wonder, "Have I changed that much that my best friend won't even talk to me?"

Another week passed by and Mr. Turner came to see Sam. "Got an update for you Sam. The trial has been set for two weeks from Monday." "Okay, what do we do between now and then?" "Well I'll begin to prepare you for the witness stand by going over potential questions that you will possibly face from the prosecution. Also, I'll go over questions that I will be asking you to make sure that we clearly articulate your version of the events as you recall them. I know you probably won't remember everything, but as much as you can we need to have a clear understanding of what it is that you can remember. Got that Sam?" "I think so. What kind of time do you think I'm facing?" "It's really hard to say. If you get a bulldog for a prosecutor, who gets a sympathetic jury, then it could be tough. Then again, who knows, they may want to plea bargain. I'm going to work on doing what is in your best interest all around." "I hear you. I just want this over with." "I know you do son. Just keep your head up and we'll work through this together."

Over the next two weeks, Mr. Turner came to see Sam just about every day as they prepared for the trial. The two of them went over the events repeatedly to make sure they hadn't missed any aspect or detail. The more they prepared the less confident Sam became in his outlook on things. "Mr. Turner, I don't stand a chance. The bottom line is, I killed a man. I may not have stabbed or shot him, but because of me his life is gone." "I understand your concern and I see your frustration, but we've got to look for the bright light at the end of the tunnel. You're right you didn't stab or shoot him so you won't be looked upon as a cold blooded murderer. You are a young man who made a mistake by drinking and choosing to drive a car. Juries have a totally different mindset for these types of trials. I'll do all I can to eliminate those who wouldn't be in our best interest to sit on your trial to give us a fighting chance to get you an outcome as favorable as possible. Get yourself some sleep, jury selection starts at 9:00 a.m. sharp." With that Sam and Mr. Turner parted company for the evening. Sam went back to his cell and picked up his Bible as had become routine for him now. "God tell me something to help me feel a little better so I can get some sleep. I've got a long day tomorrow." He began to search through the scriptures to find some comforting words. First, he read Psalm 23. This was one of the first scriptures that Phil had shown him. It was also something he had heard throughout his life but never really paid much attention to. But now, it began to hit home: *The Lord is my shepherd, I shall not want.*[17] Upon finding peace in reading Psalm 23, he looked a little further until he came upon Romans 9:14-16: *What shall we say then? Is there unrighteousness with God? God forbid. For he saith to Moses, I will have mercy on whom I will have mercy, and I will have compassion on whom I will have compassion. So then it is not of him that willeth, nor of him that runneth, but of God that showeth mercy.* Phil had told Sam once that the Bible says that *"For there is no respect of persons with God.*[18]*"* That meant that God wouldn't do something for one person that He isn't willing to do for another if He decides it is appropriate for them. Sam reasoned that if God could show mercy to Phil for committing a crime, then he too could receive mercy even though he was guilty of what he was facing. Before going to sleep Sam said this prayer: "God, I know I deserve punishment for my sins and I must be held accountable for them. I just ask for the mercy that I know you speak of in your Word to be shown to me." After praying, Sam was able to finally fall asleep.

Chapter 6

Moment of Truth

The guard came to Sam's cell about 7:30 that morning. "Your lawyer's here." Sam went to the interview room to meet with Mr. Turner as he had done many times before. Mr. Turner had a suit for Sam to wear. "Get changed, you'll be wearing this into court today." Sam gladly exchanged his bright orange county jail jumpsuit for some civilian clothing. "I had forgotten what it felt like to wear my own clothes" sighed Sam. After changing, he and Mr. Turner went over the details one last time before going into the courtroom. They sat as the potential jurors were allowed into the courtroom to begin the process of eliminating those who were not considered to be favorable to either side of the proceedings. Then the judge entered. "All rise." The judge was a stern looking older gentleman who had sat on the bench for close to 20 years. "Good morning ladies and gentlemen. We are here today to begin the jury selection process in the case of The State of Georgia v. Samuel Banks. My name is John Davis and I will be presiding over this trial. Are there any questions before we begin with this process? If not, go ahead counselor."

The prosecuting attorney went first. He began by briefly telling the potential jurors who he was and what the case before them involved. Next he began to ask a couple of general questions to feel out the jury pool. Mr. Turner objected and intervened when he deemed appropriate. After the prosecution completed their turn, Mr. Turner took his opportunity to speak on Sam's behalf. He too asked questions of the jurors and after some mini-conferences between he and the prosecuting attorney they finally agreed upon the jury to be seated. Then, a strange thing happened. "Mr. Turner, can I speak to you for a moment?" the prosecutor asked. "Sure, what is it?" "I've just got the feeling that we'd be wasting valuable time and resources by taking this to trial. The jury we've just seated doesn't give me much reason to feel good about the state's prospect's of winning. In lieu of this, let's consider a plea bargain." "I'll tell my client your feelings and get right back to you." Mr. Turner rushed to tell Sam what the prosecutor had said. "Sam, this looks good for us. He doesn't feel he'd get the conviction he's seeking, let's see what he's offering." "Go ahead Mr. Turner." Mr. Turner and the prosecutor approached the judge and asked for a brief recess to iron out the details of the proposed plea bargain. The judge granted the recess.

Sam was taken back to his cell to await word from Mr. Turner. After what seemed like forever, the guard came to escort him back to the interview room. "Sam, I've got some news for you. Vehicular homicide in this state carries a mandatory sentence of 15 years in prison. Given that you have no prior arrest record, the prosecution is willing to offer you three to five years with three years probation. The family of the victim has agreed to the terms. If we go to trial we would be taking a chance on what the jury decides and what sentence they could possibly hand out. What do you say Sam?" Although Sam wanted badly as anyone else would to be free, he had accepted responsibility and knew he had to face some punishment. With his growing relationship with God, he looked at this as an opportunity presented by God rather than complaining as he would have in the past. "Mr. Turner, I thank you for all of your hard work in helping me. I'll take the plea bargain." Mr. Turner went to the prosecuting attorney and let him know that Sam agreed to the terms. The two of them approached the bench and informed the judge of the settlement reached. He approved. Just like that, the trial was averted and

Sam was given a break from what he potentially faced. The judge then announced the plea agreement that had been reached and asked if Sam had anything to say before he formally pronounced his sentence. "Yes your honor. I have something to say. I would like to thank the family of Mr. Jenkins for being so forgiving and open to helping me to get beyond this horrible mistake. I will have to live forever knowing that because of my foolish actions, a father, husband, brother, and friend was suddenly and irresponsibly taken away from them. I just ask them to continue to find it in their hearts to forgive me as I will ask God to help me to use my mistake to help someone else from making the same mistake that I did." At that moment, Mrs. Jenkins stood up and responded to Sam. "Young man, while I hurt and suffer the loss of my husband daily, I know that God wouldn't want me to harbor unforgiveness and be resentful towards you. I agreed to the plea bargain to spare myself and my family the pain and remembrance of our anguish a trial would certainly bring. My prayer is that you will ask God to help you turn from the error of your ways so that He can be lifted up and turn this tragic set of circumstances into a triumph for His glory." Sam thanked the family once again and was led away from the courtroom. As he was walking away he said to himself "God, thank you for softening my blow. I know only you could have stepped in and done this for me. Now I'll be needing you more than ever. Please don't leave me alone." "I won't Sam. I never have and I never will. My Word promises you that." Sam faced a future of three to five years in prison. Instead of sulking over his fate, his first thought was would he get the chance to be reunited with Phil. At any rate, he knew that he had been spared what he truly had coming to him. "There is no way three to five years can equal to a man's life" said Sam. "But I'm going to do whatever I can to help someone else from making the same foolish mistake I did. Just like David is spoken of as being a man after God's own heart, I too want to be a man that can allow God to help me to overcome so that I can one day help others in return." Sam had reached a moment of truth in his life and his relationship with God. There was no turning back now.

Sam spent another week in the county jail as the paperwork was completed to finish the transfer process. Since he wasn't considered a violent offender, he was going to be sent to a minimum security facility in south Georgia. The day before his transfer Mr. Turner paid him a visit. "How are things going Sam? Just wanted to come and see you before they sent you to your next stop." "I'm doing pretty good. Trying to keep my head up and maintain a positive attitude." "That's what I wanted and was hoping to hear. While you face a stint in prison it doesn't all have to be negative. You seem like a good young man that just made a terrible mistake. I'm glad I got the chance to meet you and I wish you the best. If you ever need me for anything just give me a call." "I appreciate that Mr. Turner. I'll remember that." "Take care of yourself Sam." "I will."

The week passed by and the time had arrived for Sam to be transferred to the new facility. Although he was going from jail to prison, he looked forward just to being able to ride and see the outdoors again. "Seems like I've been in that place forever. Time just doesn't go as fast inside as it does outside." The bus ride was long, but not long enough. They arrived at the prison and it wasn't anything like Sam expected. Looking for an imposing building with tall barbed wire fences and gun towers, Sam saw a campus like facility with well manicured lawns. There were fences, but no barbed wire and no towers for guards. "What kind of prison is this?" thought Sam. "Not that I would change anything, but it sure isn't what I expected." Once the bus came to a stop, a prison guard came onboard. He shouted some instructions and ordered them to follow him off the bus. Once inside, they were given more instructions and handed a clipboard with paperwork to complete. After that, they were taken to an area where they were given their clothing and bed linens. As it was almost evening, they were taken to the cafeteria to eat dinner. Next they were escorted to their cells. Sam was placed in a one man cell which consisted of a bed, table and chair which were affixed to the floor and/or wall respectively. To his surprise there was a window. Everything kind of overwhelmed Sam to the point that he lay on his bed and looked over all that had occurred to bring him to this point. Before you knew it, he was crying himself to sleep.

Chapter 7

A New Beginning

Sam was awakened by the now too familiar sounds of guards yelling orders to one another to open cellblocks. The difference this time was he was no longer in county jail, but prison. "Wonder what to expect in here" thought Sam to himself. "Hopefully I'll meet another Phil if not Phil himself." After the count was completed to account for everyone, they were led to the cafeteria to eat breakfast. There, just like in county jail Sam kept to himself and observed his surroundings. The atmosphere didn't seem as imposing as it did in the county jail. While there were all sorts of people accused of various crimes, the guys in here were mainly low risk, non-violent offenders who had committed such crimes as fraud, forgery and of course DUI.

After breakfast, Sam was taken to meet with a counselor who "welcomed" him to the facility and told him what would be expected of him as well as what programs were available to him. He was told that he would have the choice of working in the laundry or the cafeteria. Secondly, he would be afforded the opportunity to receive alcoholics counseling if he desired. Sam reviewed all of the information and asked the counselor how long he would have to decide. "Right now" was the response given. Sam decided to work in the laundry since he didn't know anything about cooking but he opted not to take the alcoholics counseling.

Upon completion of their meeting, the counselor called for a guard who then escorted Sam to the laundry area. They entered into the area and the guard introduced him to an older gentlemen named Stan. "This is Stan. He'll take care of you." "Welcome son. What's your name?" "Sam, Sam Banks." "You nervous Sam?" "Well, kind of. I've never been in a place like this before." "I understand your concern. But unlike most 'places like this' as you call it, this isn't a typical prison. People in here are for the most part remorseful for what they've done and are trying to work on getting things back together to get it right when they get out." "That's my focus as well. I don't want any trouble, just want to do my time and be on my way." "I'm sure you won't have any problems." Stan began to show Sam around the facility and to the different machinery. He gave him lessons on how to operate the equipment. "The best teacher is practice Sam. The more you use it the more comfortable you'll become. Before you know it, you'll be an old pro."

Time passed and the weekend was upon them. Sunday arrived and Sam asked Stan if there were any church services held. "You a churchgoer son?" "Well, not really. I can count on one hand how many times I've been to church, but ever since all of this happened, I've found myself developing a relationship with God." "Is that so. A lot of young men find God when they get in this place." "I know where you're going, but unlike others who try to get close to God just in hopes of Him getting them out of their trouble, I really recognize that I need Him to help me whether I'm in trouble or not. All of my life I had been going through the motions thinking that I was 'The Man' and not needing anyone or anything. That's changed for me now. Without God I realize I would have gone out of my mind before reaching this point." "You sound like you mean that Sam. You'll have to forgive me. So many guys have done just what you mentioned and tried to run a con on God if you will. I've been back and forth in prison for most of my life and I've seen it all, but there seems to be something different about you." "There is Stan. I'm serious about this." After their brief exchange, Stan told Sam about church service and where and when it was held. "Maybe I'll come with you sometime Sam." "I'd welcome the company. This is not something I'm used to so I could use some encouragement."

Sam went into the small chapel where the services were held. Each week, a minister from one of the local churches came in to conduct the services. This week the minister's name was Rev. James Roberts. He was a middle aged gentleman who appeared to be well educated, but more importantly he seemed to be able to explain the scriptures. Although Sam knew very little for himself as he had just begun to read the Bible with any regularity, some of what the minister was saying he had run across in his reading or either Phil had shared with him during their brief time spent together. '*Trust in the Lord with all thine heart; and lean not unto thine own understanding. In all thy ways acknowledge him, and he shall direct thy paths[19]*' said Rev. Roberts. "Man, there goes that trust talk again. Trusting in God must <u>really</u> be important." The sermon ended and then Rev. Roberts asked "Have you accepted Jesus as your Lord and Savior?" Sam sat and pondered this question in his heart and mind. Although he had told God during his rehab months ago that he would accept Him, he had not really followed through with any sincere efforts to do so. Phil repeatedly told him what was required to serve God during their time spent together. Now in the very first sermon he hears he's faced with the question again. "God, I know I said it before, but this time I mean it. I want to serve you and accept your Son as my Lord and Savior." Sam got up and replied to the minister "I want to accept Him." "Come on down son. You've made the best decision of your life." Unfortunately, no one else in the small assembly chose to come to Christ, but Sam didn't let that discourage him.

Rev. Roberts took Sam aside and had a brief conversation with him after the services ended. "That was a wise decision you just made son, but can I tell you something? You didn't just make that decision on your own. If you look at the Gospel according to

John in the 15th chapter you'll find Jesus saying these words: *Ye have not chosen me, but I have chosen you, and ordained you, that ye should go and bring forth fruit, and that your fruit should remain that whatsoever ye shall ask of the Father in my name, He may give it you.*[20] So you see Sam, even though you thought about what you were about to do, it was God that put the thought in your heart to react to what He had already decided for you a long time ago. You have to believe that Jesus died for your sins and when He did, He had you in mind Sam. Even though you had yet to be created, Jesus died for you. I realize this may be a lot for you to take in all at once and probably hard to accept, but that is where faith comes in. You must have faith to trust and believe in God." Before leaving Rev. Roberts gave Sam some scriptures to read and his phone number to call him if he had any questions. "Thanks a lot Rev. Roberts. You've been a great help." "That's my job Sam. To serve God and His people."

Sam returned to his cell and looked over the scriptures Rev. Roberts had given him. However, what he said to him played back over and over in his mind: *"Ye have not chosen me, but I have chosen you.*[21]*"* To Sam, it was difficult to understand that God had actually chosen him. "I've lived my whole life with God nowhere in the picture, but His Word says that He chose me. That's mind boggling." "I know it is Sam." "Is that you God?" "Yes. I've been watching you Sam and I see that you are finally moving towards Me. Initially you thought you were ready to serve me but you regressed to your old ways. Don't feel bad, you're not the first who is guilty of that. It will be a struggle for you because the devil won't make it easy, neither will your flesh. But once you learn to depend totally upon Me you will achieve success like nothing you've ever accomplished before." "I hear you God. I intend to go all the way with you." "Good Sam. You'll need me now and always. You have been born again and now you have a new beginning in Me."

Chapter 8

Witness

Sam had begun to settle into his new "home" and his relationship with God was really beginning to blossom. He had begun to study his Bible on a daily basis and he had even grown to the point that he was sharing the good news of the gospel of Jesus Christ with some of the others. Word of Sam's profession of faith got around the prison quickly as he was a minority of one that openly practiced Christianity. One day while in the laundry, an inmate approached Sam and asked him "You that Jesus freak?" "Excuse me" said a startled Sam. "I said are you that Jesus freak that everybody is talking about?" "If you mean am I a Christian, then yes." "Why do you believe in Jesus? If He was such a great God and all, why don't He get you out of this place?" "Sir, you must understand. Jesus offers us grace and mercy and He does love us, but we have to reap the consequences of the sin that we sow and practice. Jesus isn't a genie to grant me a magic wish and free me from my physical bondage. However, He is more than able to help me through my situation and be with me so that I can be spiritually free. It took a while for me to get it and I'm still learning, but it takes faith to trust in God and serve Him. Although I can't see Him I know that He is with me because He assures me through His Word that He's always with me and that

He will never leave me alone. Following Christ doesn't come with a get out of sin free card like the get out of jail free card in Monopoly to abuse and use at our every whim. One thing though, following Him does provide something that money can't buy: joy, peace and happiness. I never truly experienced any of those until I experienced them through Christ." "I've heard all of that before, and I still don't buy it. Just doesn't make sense that a God that is supposed to be love can let so much bad stuff go in right under His nose." "God has a sovereign will that we cannot question or change. We must trust Him through the bad and the good that goes on in our life and know *'that all things work together for good to them that love God to them who are the called according to his purpose.*[22]' Before I accepted Jesus as my Lord and Savior I did things my own way. But now that He is in control, He directs my paths. Even though my actions got me in prison, He is going to see me through this and when I get out of here He will have control just as well. If you can't understand that sir, then I suggest that you, like I had to do for myself seek God in prayer and ask Him to reveal His will for your life to you." "Whatever, I don't have time for that mumbo jumbo." "Well, if you don't remember anything I said just remember that God loves you sir." The guy walked off without responding to Sam.

Stan had been observing from afar and approached Sam afterwards. "You handled him pretty good." "No Stan, I didn't handle him. The Bible says to share the good news and not keep it to myself. If someone had witnessed to me sooner, who knows where I would be now. But, I can't look at it like that, just have to keep plugging ahead." "Sam, I'm curious. How long have you been walking with God as you put it?" "Not long. God heard me ask for rest when I was in the hospital and He came and offered me rest. At first I was a skeptic and didn't think God would take the time to talk to me. But like a friend of mine told me *'for there is no respect of persons with God.*[23]' What that means is if He can or will do something for you, He doesn't have favorites to decide that He wouldn't do that or something similar for me if He knows I would benefit from it and it's in His will for my life." Sam and Stan talked until it was time to close up shop for the evening. "Why don't you come with me to the library sometimes. Maybe we could study together." "I think I'll take you up on that offer Sam."

Sam returned to his cell and reflected on the day's events. He was certainly caught off guard by the inmate who called him a "Jesus freak" and after all this time working together Stan decided to ask him something about his faith. Before going to bed, Sam said this prayer: "Father, I pray that you will be lifted up so that men can be drawn unto you. Just as you saved me from my sins God, I ask you to bless Stan and the man who approached me. Let me help them in any way I can God to give you the glory. In Jesus name Amen."

It was another Sunday and off went Sam to the chapel for services. As he entered the chapel to his surprise, he found Stan sitting there. "What are you doing here?" asked Sam. "Well young fella, I think I told you when we first met that I've been in and out of jail most of my life. Apparently I haven't been doing something right. Then you come along and you're a breath of fresh air. I've never met anyone quite like you before Sam." "Well I hope you find what it is you're looking for Stan. I'm sure you will because you're in the right place." Stan and Sam were joined by a couple of the other inmates (various inmates usually attended just to get out of a work detail and/or out of their cells). After the service the minister extended an invitation to anyone who wanted to accept Christ as his Lord and Savior. Stan got up and walked down the aisle. He accepted Christ! Sam went behind him and told the minister he already knew Jesus as his Lord and Savior, he was coming to congratulate and support Stan. The three of them hugged one another and the minister prayed this prayer: "Father, we thank you for looking upon us with your love and kindness. I ask that you would take Stan and keep him close to you and in your strong right hand. Bless Sam to be a friend in need to him Lord and allow them to encourage one another. Protect them from the certain attacks of the enemy. We thank you in the name of your Son and our Savior Jesus Christ. Amen." After leaving the chapel, Stan and Sam went to the library to study the Bible and Sam began to help Stan as he started his walk with the Lord. "How can I ever repay you Sam?" "You don't owe me anything but love. The Bible tells us so."

Sam and Stan embarked on their joint journey into Christianity. Although Sam was a new Christian himself, he was Stan's mentor – just as Stan had mentored him when he first arrived at the prison and began to work in laundry. "Well Sam, I got to teach you something and you get to teach me something." "It's my pleasure Stan. But remember, it's not me but it's God that is going to be leading and guiding both of us. The Bible says that '*neither is he that planteth any thing, neither is he that watereth, but God giveth the increase.*[24]' That means that one person shared Jesus Christ with you, another person comes along to help you understand more about what you were told about Christ but neither of those persons is responsible or gets the credit for you accepting Him as your Savior and blessing your walk with Him after doing so. It is God and God alone that keeps us while we are walking with Him and He deserves all of the honor and glory." "I get it Sam. God is just going to use you to help me like He used your friend Phil to help you."

Chapter 9

Crisis

Sam and Stan engrossed themselves in seeking after God and studying His Word. Stan found fascinating things in the Bible on his own and with Sam's help. "All of these interesting things are in the Bible and I've chosen to ignore them for all this time. What a fool I've been." "Don't beat yourself up Stan. We have to thank God for the time that we do get to spend in fellowship with Him. Better to get to know Him than to not have met Him at all." "That is so true Sam." The two of them became known around the prison as the "Bible Boys" as they were always either reading or quoting scripture.

One day Sam reported to work and Stan was not there. This was highly unusual as Stan was a stickler for punctuality. Sam sought out the first guard he could find. "Where's Stan?" he asked. "Haven't you heard?" replied the guard. "Heard what?" "Stan suffered a stroke last night. The doctor on call couldn't give him the help he needed, so he was rushed to the hospital." "You've got to be kidding. Stan looked the picture of health." "I don't know what else to tell you. Someone will be in shortly to replace him. Guess you'll have to train him." Sam faced his first test as a Christian since his trial. "God, why did this have to happen? Stan was just beginning to walk with you and getting to know you." Upon hearing Sam, God spoke to him in as stern a manner as He ever had before. "I am the Lord thy God. I work in mysterious ways. I must be trusted and not questioned Sam." "God I hear you and I understand who you are. It's just that Stan had wasted so much of his life and then he finally accepted your Son as His Lord and Savior. Why did this have to happen now?" "A better question is why didn't it happen sooner" said God. "Because of my grace and mercy I kept Stan until I sent you to him and he was able to come to know Me personally. How would he be fairing if he were in this state without Me?" "I never thought about it like that God. I repent." "I forgive you Sam."

Sam went into prayer and fasting on Stan's behalf. "God receive my efforts on behalf of Stan and look upon him through eyes of mercy" Sam prayed. He did this faithfully for two weeks. Then one day as he was reporting to work, Sam was met by one of the guards. "Got some bad news for you Sam. Stan died last night." Sam was overcome with emotion. He ran the gamut from sadness to anger. He knew that the Bible says to *Anger but sin not.*[25]" But Sam was frustrated. His friend had just come to know Christ and was at the beginning of what seemed to him a beautiful relationship. And just like that, he was gone. Sam was angry. "God how could you allow this to happen? Why didn't you give Stan a chance? I fasted and I prayed and I thought you would heal him? What happened God?" Before Sam could rattle off another question God interrupted him and said *Shall he that contendeth with the Almighty instruct Him? He that reproveth God, let him answer it. Gird up thy loins now like a man. I will demand of thee, and declare thou unto me. Hast thou an arm like God? Canst thou thunder with a voice like him?*[26]" Immediately Sam recognized the error of his ways. He fell flat on his face before God and uttered these words: "Forgive your servant God. I beg your forgiveness. You are the Lord God Almighty. You and You alone. With all that I have I worship you. I reverence your holy name and render glory and praises to you for what you've done. Thank you God for sparing Stan long enough to come to the knowledge of you and your Son Jesus. I bless your holy name." Sam got up and began to cry.

Two weeks passed and Sam received a letter in the mail. It was from a young lady in Washington, D.C. "I wonder who this is?" He opened the letter and discovered that it was from Stan's granddaughter. Stan had only mentioned his family sparingly. During the time Sam knew him no one had come to visit him. However, he had spoken highly of Sam to his granddaughter. The letter read: "Dear Mr. Banks. I know you don't know me, but I'm Stan Benson's granddaughter Tracy. He has told me a lot about you. Most importantly he said you introduced him to Christ. I am a Christian, but most of the family had turned it's back on my grandfather. My dad is his son. Even though they were estranged, I believe my father and grandfather still loved one another. Anyway, I know you couldn't make it to his funeral, so I thought I'd enclose a program for your review. I attend college in Washington, D.C., but our family lives in Memphis, Tennessee. That's where my grandfather was from. In closing, I'd like to say thank you again for showing my grandfather the love of Jesus so that he too could accept Him as his Lord and Savior. Your sister in Christ, Tracy Benson." Sam began to cry as he recalled the brief time he spent with Stan. However, instead of shedding tears of sadness, he was glad that God had used him to help someone to know Him. "I sure miss Stan, but it's good to know he accepted Christ rather than leaving this world without having known Him."

Chapter 10

Challenge

Sam was introduced to the new guy that was sent to help him in the laundry to replace Stan. It was a young man who was imprisoned for burglary. His name was Jeff and he was just 22 years old. "How's it going man. My name is Sam. And you are?" "Jeff. That's all you need to know." "Don't want any friction, just want to get to know who I'm working with." "Just show me what I need to do and let that be it. I don't need no friends, alright?" Sam began the task of showing Jeff the machinery and equipment just as Stan had shown him. It seemed strange being in the laundry without Stan. Although they were together only a short time, it seemed to Sam like an eternity especially after Stan accepted Christ and they spent time together away from the laundry as well. Now, here was this young 'tough guy' who was sent to replace Stan and Sam was in a quandary as to his approach. Should he just teach Jeff the job and back off as Jeff had made it clear to do, or should he show Jeff the love of Christ in hopes of winning him over as he had done with Stan.

The days passed and Jeff would come to work and do what was required – no more, no less. He barely said two words to Sam during the day and was short whenever he did have something to say. Finally, Sam grew tired of this and asked God how should he approach the situation. "God, what should I do. I know your Word says to spread your gospel, but what do I do with a person like Jeff?" God said to Sam: *"Let your let so shine before men that they may see your good works, and glorify your Father which is in heaven.²⁷"* I understand God, letting him see my life is better than anything I could say to him."

The next morning when he arrived for work, Sam spoke to Jeff. "What's up man? Did you work out last night?" "Nope" replied Jeff. "Well, what did you do?" "Nothing, what's it to you?" "I was just asking because sometimes after dinner I go and study the Bible. I used to read with Stan before he passed away, but now I read alone. I was just wondering if maybe you'd like to join me sometimes." "Man, you must be crazy. I ain't reading no Bible. That ain't for me." "The Bible is open and available for all to read Jeff. If you change your mind, just let me know." "I never read the Bible before and besides why should I?" "Well Jeff, the Bible says *'thy word is a lamp unto my feet, and a light unto my path.²⁸'* What that means is the Word of God guides our footsteps and shows us the way to go and just as important the way not to go in life. Without it we make more mistakes than we would with it. Don't get me wrong, I still mess up, it's just that now I have something to get me back on the right track. You understand." "I guess so, but I've always handled my own business and done things my way." "So did I Jeff. But one day I realized that without Jesus Christ, I was messing up all of my business and making terrible decisions regardless of how it seemed to me that they were turning out. Without Christ, no matter how successful we think we are or appear to be, nothing we do or accomplish is truly for our good without Him in lives. Whatever it is we do will always be in vain. Just remember if you ever change your mind, I'll be here." "Yeah, whatever."

Sam and Jeff continued to work together. Sam tried his best to let his light shine and show Christ while Jeff maintained his rough exterior and resisted all of Sam's overtures. One night after returning to his cell Sam was reading. He had asked God again about ways in which he could go about trying to reach Jeff as he had

51

reached Stan. Before you know it is was time for lights out. As Sam lay in his bed he began to hear the voice of God: "Sam, don't feel bad or as if you've failed. You must remember that my Son Jesus was sent to save man from his sins and while he lived a perfect, sinless life, not everyone chose to receive Him. He was rejected by His own, so you must know that everyone will not receive you." "I understand God. I just wish that Jeff would come to know you as I have. Things would be so much easier for him, especially in here."

Sunday came and Sam went to the chapel for services. He had become familiar with all of the ministers that rotated coming to lead the service on each Sunday. This Sunday a minister that he particularly liked was coming, Rev. George Clark. Sam really enjoyed him and could relate to him because he too was a young man, barely 30 years old. After the service he went to Rev. Clark to have a chat with him. "Rev. Clark, I really enjoyed you today." "Thank you Sam, just trying to do what God would have me to do." "Rev. Clark, I have a situation I need some help with. The young man that works in the laundry with me doesn't know Christ. I've attempted to share Christ with him and more importantly I've done as the Word tells us and let my light shine before him. He still doesn't respond and doesn't seem as if he's going to. After praying about the situation I heard God tell me that not everyone was going to receive Jesus and that He was rejected while He walked here on the earth. I guess my problem is I don't understand why I was able to get to know Christ even though I did so much wrong and others won't get to know or accept Him." "Well Sam, you've asked a question that's going to be asked throughout the ages. The one thing I can tell you is that we must never question God's decision making or His sovereign will. There will be times when things are difficult to explain or reason, but God works in mysterious ways. God's Word tells us that '*no man can serve two masters for either he will hate the one and love the other.*[29]' There are some people that are going to choose to continue serving the world rather than serving God. You got to receive Christ because you chose to serve Him in your heart and you accepted His Son. That's the difference Sam." "I hear you, but it's a hard pill to swallow."

Chapter 11

Opportunity

Before you know it, a year had gone by. Sam "celebrated" the anniversary by thanking God for keeping him and looking forward to getting the next two under his belt. He got up and prepared for work as usual. Upon arriving in the laundry he was greeted by a guard. "Banks, come with me." Sam was perplexed by this and asked where he was being taken. "To the counselor's office." "What for?" asked Sam. "I don't know. You'll find out when you get there." Sam anxiously sat outside the counselor's office. He went over and over in his mind what he could possibly want. He knew he hadn't done anything to get himself in any trouble. Then, he concluded that maybe Jeff had complained about his witnessing. "I sure hope I don't get in trouble for that!" thought Sam. The door opened and the counselor appeared. "Come in Sam, I've been expecting you." Sam went in and took a seat. "What's going on? Why am I here?" Sam asked nervously. "Well Sam, we've been monitoring you since your arrival as we do all the other inmates. You have been exceptional in your behavior, work ethic and overall attitude since you've been here. As a result, we consider certain inmates for early parole and your name has come up for consideration." "Early parole. Are you serious?" "Yes I am Sam. What would happen is you would go before a state pardon and parole board, consisting of 3-5 members and they would look at your case and take all things into consideration. They then make a ruling which would be given in about two weeks. The group is meeting with inmates from our prison on next Thursday. I wanted to give you time to prepare yourself. You would like to be considered wouldn't you?" "Of course!" "Good, then go back to the laundry and we'll keep in touch."

Sam walked back to the laundry beaming a 1,000 watt smile. He had been following Christ for a little over a year now and without warning, it seemed as if a miracle had just fallen into his lap. Being careful not to put the cart before the horse, Sam came off of his natural high and thought to himself "I won't get happy too quick. I'll wait until it's time to really celebrate and then I'll rejoice. But whatever happens I just thank God that He has given me this opportunity."

The next week seemed to take forever to arrive as Sam anxiously awaited his day. He had thought about what the counselor told him he could possibly expect and even "rehearsed" the moment over and over again in his mind. Not wanting to be too anxious, he remembered something he read in the book of Philippians '*be careful for nothing, but in every thing by prayer and supplication with thanksgiving let your requests be made known unto God.*[30]' Sam continued to prepare himself but most importantly, he said this prayer: "Dear God, I thank you for this opportunity that I know I am not worthy of. Now that you have presented it before me, I just ask that you would give me favor with men and speak on my behalf that whatever your will for my life would be done. In Jesus name I pray, Amen." With that, Sam went to sleep.

Thursday arrived and not a moment too soon. "I don't know if I could have waited one more day. The suspense was killing me!" said Sam. The guard came to escort him to the counselor's office. "Ready for your big day Sam?" asked the counselor. "I sure am. I've been waiting for this ever since you told me about it." "Just remember to take your time in responding to their questions and stay calm. I know you'll do fine Sam." "Thanks, thanks for everything." "My pleasure Sam." Sam entered the room and there were five people – three women and two men, seated behind a long table. They all had a copy of his file before them. "Sit down Mr. Banks." Sam sat down and looked at each of them to try to gauge their demeanor. He felt was a bit nervous, but he was ready. After a moment or two, one of the ladies began by saying "I guess you know why we're here. Would you like to say anything before we begin?" "No ma'am. I would just like for things to get underway." The questions began to come at Sam as if being shot from a machine gun in rapid fire fashion. He was able to keep his composure and do an admirable job of responding. After about 30 minutes one of the gentlemen said "I think we've covered all that we need and we have enough information. You'll be hearing from us. Thank you for your time." "Thank each of you for taking the time to listen to me" replied Sam. By this time it was lunch and Sam went to the cafeteria to eat, but he wasn't really hungry so he just picked over his food. He was thinking "Did I really do a good job? When will I hear from them? What are they going to decide?" At that moment, Sam stopped and remembered what Matthew 6:34 says: *'Take therefore no thought for the morrow, for the morrow shall take thought for the things of itself. Sufficient unto the day is the evil thereof.'* "No need worrying myself about something I have no control over. I'll let God handle it and stay out of His way."

An entire month passed and Sam still hadn't received word regarding his pardon. "Even if it's no I'd like for someone to tell me something. The wait to find out is killing me!" As he finished his morning duties, a guard approached him and told him the counselor wanted to see him after lunch. "Can I go to see him now?" asked an anxious Sam. "No, after lunch is what he said." "Alright then. I've waited this long a few more minutes won't hurt." Sam went to lunch and scarfed his meal down so that he could hurry to the counselor's office. He sat outside and waited impatiently as he heard him in his office on a phone call. "Hurry up" thought Sam. Just as his patience was about to run bare, the counselor hung up and came to the door. "Come in Sam. I've been expecting you." Sam entered the room not really knowing what to expect the counselor to say. Regardless of what he said, Sam just wanted to hear something. Not knowing was driving him crazy. "Well Sam, I received word back from the pardons and parole board regarding you. They denied your early parole. I'm sorry Sam. You'll be eligible again, I just don't know when." "Do you know why they denied me?" "To be honest no. I thought you had everything in your favor, you had exemplary reviews and all of the guards spoke highly of you. It just wasn't meant to be now. Don't hang your head though. I'm sure next time, you'll get it." Sam left the office very depressed. He was certain that he would be getting out of prison. Now he would have to stay. Upon going back to the laundry, Jeff broke his usual silent treatment. "Well, you get parole?" asked Jeff. "No, I got turned down." "I know that would make me mad and upset, but you're supposed to be this big time Christian. How come you seem so low. Didn't you say that regardless of your situation, as long as you had Jesus, everything was alright. I knew you were a bunch of talk." At first Sam got angry, then after thinking on Jeff's words he realized he was right. Philippians 4:11 says *'I have learned whatsoever state I am in therewith to be content.'* Now was put up or shut up time. He had worked with Jeff for months and not been able to win him over to Christ. This would be a perfect opportunity for Christ to be glorified in his life and he could show a powerful example of trusting in Him. "Jeff, you're right. I can't lie to you and say that I'm not disappointed, but just as I've been trusting in the Lord before now I will continue to trust Him. His will is going to go forth regardless of what I do or say and I just have to accept it. Nevertheless, I will trust Him."

Sunday came and Sam prepared to go to the chapel. As was his custom, he took his Bible and a notepad to jot down tidbits from the sermon. Just as he was walking up the hallway, seemingly out of nowhere Jeff appeared. "Thought I'd go check the chapel out today" said Jeff. "You're more than welcome to join me." "I really didn't think you were going to go today with what happened earlier this week." "To be honest with you, I didn't feel like going but I've come too far with God to turn back now.

Besides, He helped me make it through a whole year in prison, I know He can keep me through the remainder of my sentence." Jeff and Sam went off to the chapel for the service. As always, Sam enjoyed the service. Jeff being new didn't know what to expect so he sat and half heartedly participated. Afterwards he went to Sam and asked him "Why do you keep coming here?" "Because I recognize that I need Jesus to make it and that without Him I'd be lost and hopeless. With Him I continue to have hope." "Hope in what? Don't you realize you were denied parole?" "Yes I do realize that. But I still have hope, not in man but in Jesus Christ. The hope that I have is that through Him I can have the victory in spite of seeming defeat. Jeff, the way things work with God are the total opposite to the manner in which they work in the world. Even though the parole board said no to me regarding my physical freedom, they have no control over my spiritual joy. Because of that I am free through Jesus and I have joy that the parole board, the warden or any other entity for that matter cannot control. That's what I have hope in." "I never knew somebody could be happy being locked up." "Jeff, did you know that there are people who walk the streets everyday that are more locked up than you and I?" "What do you mean?" "They are locked up spiritually because they don't have freedom from their sins. As a result they are in bondage to their sin instead of having the peace of mind that comes from having Jesus Christ setting you free from your sin." "I never knew all of this before." "Neither did I until I came into the knowledge of who Jesus Christ is and what He had done for us. The thing is you have to accept Him for yourself. No one else can do it on your behalf and no one else can be saved for you." "I used to hear my mama talk about God and Jesus and go to church when I was a kid. She never forced me to go so I didn't. Our situation in life never looked as if God cared about us to me. We were always one step away from being put outdoors and we never had much money. I figured why bother worshipping a God that is going to keep you broke." "But Jeff I would say to you that God kept you from being totally broke. You said yourself you were always one step from being put outdoors. Who do you think it was that kept you from being outdoors? Did you ever think about that?" "I always thought it was my mama coming through." "Well, it was God enabling your mother to come through so that you wouldn't meet the fate you thought you would. Jeff, God works in mysterious ways. What may seem like a hopeless situation to us is a perfect opportunity for God to be glorified by seeing us through." The two of them talked for so long before they realized it, it was time for the evening meal. "Well Jeff I really enjoyed talking to you, I'll see you in the morning at work." "Yeah man. Thanks for telling me so much that I didn't know." "That's what we have to do. Share the good news of Jesus Christ."

Chapter 12

Questions and Answers

Now that God had given Sam the breakthrough necessary to begin to minister to Jeff, it seemed as if he was determined to make up for all those months of silence as he began to ask Sam question after question: How long have you been a Christian? When you were in the hospital did you ever feel like giving up? How did you feel when you got sent to prison?, etc. Jeff was full of questions but Sam was not always prepared to answer him. "Jeff, I'll have to be honest with you. I'm such a new Christian myself that some of the questions you are asking me I don't know the answers. Write down your questions and come with me to the chapel and we'll ask the minister." "I don't really trust preachers" said Jeff. "Why not?" asked Sam wondrously. "Because when I was a little boy my mama used to go to church it seemed like almost everyday. She would always say how she trusted in the Lord and would give her money to the church. Everybody in my neighborhood that went to church gave money. But we never benefited from it. All I could see was the preacher getting over on people. He had the nice clothes and the nice car. We were on the bus and wearing second hand clothes or something my mama made for the most part. For that reason, I don't like or trust them." Sam was really at a loss for words. He had not begun to deal with ministers himself until he came to know Christ and it was the prison ministers that he had relationships with. To be honest, his image of ministers was the same as that of Jeff's before accepting Christ. Now what would he say. While he searched his mind for the words he recalled a scripture he read dutifully as he prepared for his parole board hearing *"Take no thought how or what ye shall speak for it shall be given you in that same hour what ye shall speak. For it is not ye that speak, but the Spirit of your Father which speaketh in you.*[31]*"* At that very moment Sam simply said to Jeff: "The Word of God tells us that *'man shall not live by bread alone but by every word that proceedeth out of the mouth of God.*[32]*'* Because of this Jeff, even if it appears that a minister is 'getting over' if you will on the congregation he will suffer dire consequences. And in spite of what we may or may not have as long as we have Jesus Christ in our life we have everything we need through Him."

Sunday came and Jeff contemplated whether or not he should go to the chapel as Sam had invited him. "I just don't know. Sam seems cool and all but I just can't be too sure" he reasoned. At that moment, Sam came by. "How's it going Jeff? You coming to chapel today?" "I guess so." The two of them went to the chapel. Right before they entered, Sam said to Jeff "I urge you to allow the Lord to speak to your heart today. Don't 'listen' to the minister, but rather look to hear from God." "How can I not listen to the preacher when he's the one that is going to be talking?" asked Jeff. "What I mean by that is you need to listen to see if he is speaking what lines up with the Word of God and if so you can receive it. If it isn't then you don't receive it. The Bible tells us to *'study to show thyself approved a workman unto God that needeth not be ashamed rightly dividing the word of truth.*[33]*'* We should study God's Word for ourselves and not just depend on a preacher or anyone else for that matter to tell us and take their word for it. We need to know for ourselves. A friend I met in the county jail told me that *'God is a rewarder of them that diligently seek him.*[34]*'* You need to make the decision for yourself Jeff. Will you seek after him or not."

After finishing his sermon, as always the minister made an invitation to those in attendance to accept Christ. Jeff sat there and pondered whether or not he should go up and accept Christ. Sam had witnessed to him many times and one thing that he did remember Sam telling him was we can't waste time or play around because Christ is coming back soon and the Bible says *"that day and hour knoweth no man, no, not the angels which are in heaven, but the Father only.*[35]*"* Just as the minister was about to close the service, Jeff sprang from his seat. "I want to accept Jesus as my Lord and Savior." Sam looked up with excitement and happiness. God had used him to lead two people to Christ. "Thank you Lord for helping me to let my light shine before men so that you can be glorified" thought Sam.

After the service, Sam congratulated Jeff and told him he was happy that he had made the decision to accept Christ. "If it hadn't been for you I probably never would have accepted Christ" said Jeff. "God deserves all the glory Jeff. He could have used anybody, for some reason He used me. But the important thing is that you yielded to Him. That's all that matters." "You're going to have to help me a lot because I don't know too much about church stuff" Jeff sighed. "It's not about church Jeff, but rather it's about having a relationship with Jesus Christ. Think about it, we don't go to a traditional church because you and I are incarcerated right now. But we are able to experience Him in chapel and out of chapel. That's more important than any 'church stuff' as you put it. Just remember that even when you do get released from here you need to go to church because God tells us in His Word we should *'not forsaking the assembling of ourselves together, as the manner of some is; but exhorting one another and so much the more, as ye see the day approaching.*[36]*'"* "Man, there's a lot to this isn't it?" "Yes there is, but there is a lot of stuff going on in the world as well. We have to choose which is best for us to follow after – the things of the world or the things of God."

Chapter 13

Confrontation

Sam now had a new friend in Jeff to share the joy of following Christ. Just as he had with Stan, the two of them spent countless hours reading the scriptures in the library and the laundry as well. They were fixtures in the chapel on Sundays and the "Bible Boys" moniker had resurfaced in lieu of Sam now having a new partner in Christianity. Sam's second "anniversary" of his incarceration was just weeks away. "Seems like the days turn into weeks, the weeks into months and the months into years in this place" moaned Sam. "God has brought me this far, I know He won't leave me."

The weekend came and Sam was going to shoot some basketball. Just as he was headed for the recreation area a guard approached: "Banks, you've got a visitor." Sam hadn't had any visitors since his mother and sisters came to visit him from Baltimore and that had been a month ago. "Who is this?" wondered Sam. After arriving in the visitation area, he was shocked to see Tim seated. He had written Tim and shared his new found relationship with Christ. But the last time they saw one another, Tim left the room abruptly when Sam began to talk about Christ. "Long time no see" said Sam as he entered the room. "I know. I've gotten your letters. Just not a letter writing type of guy. You understand" said Tim. "I guess so" replied Sam. "So, you still on your little Jesus kick I see" smirked Tim. "Jesus kick? No Tim, this is real. I have accepted Jesus as my Lord and Savior." "Man, let that go! Don't you see you're still locked up. Why didn't you get early parole last year if you had it so hooked up with God as you say you do." "Tim, I received grace and mercy when I didn't face a trial and the possibility of the full sentence I was facing. I can't dare complain about God not allowing me early parole when He had already done that on my behalf." "I see you're still tripping. Don't you realize that you are locked up and in a hopeless situation?" "That's where you're wrong. My situation is not hopeless because I'm not facing it alone. It would be hopeless without Christ. But with Him I have hope and I know that He is going to see me through." "You have lost your mind altogether. You really believe that some miracle is going to come out of this." "The miracle is that I still have peace of mind. Don't you realize I was in an accident that took a man's life? Without Christ I would have lost my mind and been hopeless. With Him it's the total opposite." "Whatever man, you believe what you want to believe. I just hadn't seen you in a while and thought I'd drop by. I see things haven't changed. When you come back to your senses let me know." "I have my senses, but I'll keep in touch and keep you in prayer." "Whatever."

Sam left the visitation area not knowing how to look at his meeting with Tim. He knew one thing though – he was sure now more than ever before that he was in his walk with God for the long haul. As he sat reflecting, Jeff walked up. "Where were you? We waited for 30 minutes then we decided to go ahead and start playing." "I had a visit from an old friend of mine." "Is that so?" "Yes. It was an interesting meeting." "How so?" "Well, he seems to believe that I am just trying to use Christ if you will because of the fact that I'm locked up." "He can talk to me. If anybody can help me to change, they've got to be legit." "I appreciate that Jeff, but I can't worry about it. I still count him as my friend and I will keep him before the Lord in prayer so that one day he too can come to know Jesus Christ as his Lord and Savior. But the scriptures say *'whosoever therefore will be a friend of the world is the enemy of God.*[37]*'* One thing I know I can say without a doubt is that once I was an enemy of God because I didn't know Him and now that I've come out of darkness into His light, I don't want to go back even if it comes at the expense of losing Tim's friendship." "You sound serious." "I am serious. God made it clear to us that He is serious about His relationship with us when He sent His only begotten Son Jesus to die on the cross for our sins. A God that would do that for someone who didn't even acknowledge Him or His love until just over two years ago and loved me until I was able to recognize Him, I'd be foolish to turn away from. The Bible says that *'the fool hath said in his heart, there is no God.*[38]*'* While I may not be the smartest person around, I definitely don't want to be counted in the number of fools that don't acknowledge God and His Son." "I hear you man. I'm glad that I know Him for myself now. It feels as if the weight of the world is off my shoulders." "Well Jeff, remember we read once that God tells us to *'take my yoke upon you and learn of me for I am meek and lowly in heart and ye shall find rest unto your souls. For my yoke is easy and my burden is light.*[39]*'* So you're quite correct in saying that you feel like the weight of the world is off of your shoulders. The world bogs you down with its cares and worries and then sin is like a 10,000 ton cherry on top of all of that. But in Jesus Christ we have freedom, peace and liberty because He makes it easy for us by taking care of every aspect of our lives – as long as we allow Him to do that and don't interrupt Him by not exercising faith and getting in the way. *'Where the Spirit of the Lord is, there is liberty.*[40]*'* I've been in darkness and misery all of my life. Now that I've come to know Christ I want to stay with Him and always be in His presence. That's not only the best place to be, it's the safest place to be." "You're right about that Sam. Ever since I've established my relationship with Him my life has changed so much for the better. I know that when I get out of this place I will have a different mindset about things than I did before." "Jeff it all starts in the mind. *'Let this mind be in you which was also in Christ Jesus.*[41]*'* Our mindset is totally worldly because we are born into

64

sin and we have this flesh that constantly comes against our efforts to serve God. Romans 8:6-7 states: *'For to be carnally minded is death but to be spiritually minded is life and peace. Because the carnal mind is enmity against God for it is not subject to the law of God, neither indeed can be.'* So you see Jeff because God doesn't force His will upon us or make us robot like, we have to have the mind like Jesus did when He too walked in the flesh and give our will over to God to let Him have the lead role in our lives. Without Him we will fail miserably trying to do things on our own." "You're so right. I'm glad to know that I don't have to go it alone when I get out of here."

Chapter 14

Letting Go

Six months elapsed and Jeff was eligible for release. Although he had gotten in more than his fair share of trouble as a youth, he had most of it removed from his record by doing community service. As a result, even though he was charged with burglary it was "technically" his first offense. "Sam, the time has come for me to move on. I can't tell you how much I appreciate you being patient with me and allowing God to break down the walls I had built up so that He could use you to reach me." "That's what it's all about Jeff. God shows us patience that we couldn't possibly match. How could I not be patient and share His love with others when He extended grace and mercy towards me." "I've encountered a lot of people in my life that have said they were Christians but you are the first person that has really shown me the unconditional love of Jesus Christ." "To God be the glory and honor Jeff. Just glad to be used so that others can get to know what I've come to know." A few days later, Jeff was gone.

The night Jeff was released, Sam sat in his cell and thought. He wasn't really thinking about the remainder of his sentence (which at this point was less than six months), but rather he was thinking about all of the friends that he had made since he had come to know Christ. It seemed as if just as they were getting close and comfortable in their friendship, they moved on. And in Stan's case, passed away. Sam began to ask God about this. "God, why is it that you allow me to meet this people. In Phil's case, he ministered to me and in Stan and Jeff's case you allowed me to minister to them. Then just as our relationship should have been taking off, you took them away from me. I am getting tired of letting go of the people that mean so much to me. Why does this keep happening?"

Sunday arrived and as always Sam went to chapel. The minister this week was a new minister that he had never seen before. He was a middle aged gentleman named Rev. Carl Smith. Sam was really anxious to get to chapel because he was hoping and expecting God to speak to him in regards to the question he had asked earlier in the week. The sermon while powerful, didn't strike Sam as what he thought he would hear. Rev. Smith's sermon was taken from Matthew 14:22-33, as he talked about the miracle of Jesus walking on the water and allowing Peter to do the same until his faith failed him and he began to sink. While the sermon was powerful, it just didn't seem to strike a chord with Sam. He had asked a question of God and expected and answer that he didn't feel he received.

Later that evening as he sat in his cell, he reviewed some of the notes he had taken during the sermon. Once again he called out to God to ask the question: "Why is it that everyone I seem to get close with I have to let go of them." "Because you only need to draw close to me." "God is that you?" "Yes it's me. I heard your question. I want you to have faith in me and me alone. That's was the message I attempted to get to you through today's sermon Sam. I put Phil in your life for but a moment because that was the moment you needed him and I gave you what you needed to have through him. Remember how he just approached you during breakfast when you were initially jailed and instead of trouble which you thought you would find you found someone who shared my love?" "Yes I do Lord." "My Word says to '*be not forgetful to entertain strangers for thereby some have entertained angels unawares.*[42]' I sent Phil to you to get you prepared for what you were about to go through and what I was preparing to use you for as well." "I'm getting the picture now" replied Sam. "You were ordering my steps just as your Word said you would." "Of course I was and I am continuing to do so. I knew that you would meet Stan in the laundry and I used you to minister to him and He accepted My Son as his Lord and Savior. It was no coincidence that you came into his life when he did, because as you see he died shortly thereafter. I allowed you to spend a little time with Jeff because he had never experienced me just as you hadn't. I needed to get his heart and mind ready for when he had to separate from your presence so that he would know he could depend on me when he faced adversities in life. Do you understand Sam?" "Yes God, I believe I see your plan unfolding. I just want to know what you have in store for me." "Be patient Sam. Know that '*I am with you always even unto the end of the world.*[43]' Also remember that '*no good thing will I uphold from them that walk uprightly.*[44]' Continue to walk in My Will and study My Word Sam. You must have faith and trust in Me." Just as suddenly as God began to speak, He stopped.

Sam began to serve God and study the scriptures with a renewed vigor. He had heard from God and had a renewed assurance from on high that He was on the right path. Sam was excited about what God was doing in his life and how he had seen so much change for the better in and around him. As his release date was fast approaching, he began to prepare résumés and letters to send out to prospective employers explaining his situation. The counselor and some of the ministers who came to preach in the chapel wrote letters of recommendation on his behalf. Sam was praying that his efforts would not be in vain and that someone would have mercy and give him the opportunity he so desperately desired and needed to get back on his feet once he was released. "Somebody's just got to give me a second chance. If God can do it, then man has to recognize I deserve the opportunity" thought Sam. As his release date drew closer, he had yet to have any positive feedback. Sam began to get discouraged and was losing hope. It was at that moment that he remembered that the Word of God says: '*Every good gift and every perfect gift is from above, and cometh down from the Father of lights.*[45]' He then began to get encouraged and thought to himself "If God can give me favor with man and spare me from the prison sentence that I truly deserved then I know without a doubt He can and will prepare a situation that He knows is ideal for me to be in so that He can be glorified."

Chapter 15

Freedom

Three long years had finally passed and it was time for Sam to be released from prison. "Hallelujah!" shouted Sam as he arose on his release date. He looked back over the time that he had spent in prison and remembered how God had brought him from the minute he arrived down to this very moment. He reflected on meeting Phil in the county jail and their brief friendship; he wistfully remembered his friendship with Stan. Lastly he marveled at how God broke through the rough exterior Jeff had built up over the years to penetrate his heart with His Word and how they were able to fellowship with one another. Now after all of that it was time for Sam to go. "Come with me Banks" said the guard. "You're getting your walking papers today aren't you Banks?" "Yes I am and I don't ever want to see a place like this again." "I know what you mean. It's can be pretty depressing in here. You seem to be one of the few that I can say will probably do the right thing on the outside." "As long as I follow Christ, I will do what's right." After his brief exchange with the guard Sam completed some paperwork and gathered all of his belongings to get ready for his trip back to Atlanta. He considered going to Baltimore to be with his mother and sisters for awhile, but decided to stay where he had planted his roots and trust God to be with him as he got off to his new start.

Although they last parted on uneasy terms, Tim had offered to come pick Sam up from prison. He decided to ride the bus to relax and gather his thoughts before he got back to Atlanta. Sam enjoyed seeing the countryside during his trip. "It seems like forever since I've seen normal sights. Those bars get old quick." About 45 minutes into the trip the country landscape gave way to skyscrapers and the familiar sights and sounds of the hustle and bustle of city life. Sam was back in Atlanta. His first order of business was contacting his probation officer who would direct him to a halfway house. He was to spend his first six weeks there as he got acclimated to being out of prison. After calling the probation officer Sam took in his surroundings. The last thing he remembered was standing in the line with Tim at the nightclub. He had gotten so drunk, he could recall none of the events that occurred while he was in the club nor could he remember being stopped by the police or the accident that led to all of this. Regardless of all those things Sam was enjoying his freedom. "Man, there is no price you can put on being free. I don't ever want to be locked up like that again. Thank you God for seeing fit to shorten my sentence and allowing me this opportunity."

Sam hailed a cab and got a ride to go see his probation officer. He arrived at the office but to Sam's chagrin he had been called away on an emergency. "How long before he gets back?" he asked the receptionist. "I can't say for sure. Just have a seat and wait Mr. Banks. He should be back shortly." There was all kinds of activity going on around Sam. People yelling back and forth at one another across the office, doors opening and closing, arguments with those on the phone. "Man this is crazy. I sure wish he would hurry up and get here so I can see him and leave" said Sam.

An hour passed and Sam continued to impatiently wait for his probation officer to return. Just as he began to read a magazine a gentleman approached him "You Sam Banks?" "Yes sir and you are?" "Matthews, Bill Matthews. Come this way." Sam got up and followed Mr. Matthews to his cluttered desk. "Sorry about the wait. Had a guy call with an emergency I had to go and take care of." "No problem, I understand. You probably get a lot of those."

"Sometimes. Just a minute while I familiarize myself with your file." Mr. Matthews took a few minutes to read through Sam's file. He sat it down and looked over his glasses at Sam. "You are an engineer I see. "Yes sir." "What plans do you have now that you're out of prison?" "Well, I submitted résumés to a number of companies a couple of months before my release, unfortunately I haven't had any positive responses." "It is tough when you first get out, but we'll help you get on your feet." "I appreciate that. I could use all the help that I can get." Sam and Mr. Matthews continued talking for another 30 minutes or so. After their meeting was over Mr. Matthews offered Sam a ride to the halfway house. Sam took him up on the offer. "Do you have any family here Sam?" "No, my mother and sisters are my only family and they are in Baltimore. I came to Atlanta to go to school and ended up staying here after graduation. I've been here close to 10 years now." "I see. Well, if there is anything you need until you get settled just let me know. I'm here to help as long as you do what I ask of you." "Don't worry Mr. Matthews, I will."

Sam arrived at the halfway house. Once again, just as in county jail and prison, he didn't know what to expect. The house was huge and seemed as if it had a million rooms there were so many doors. Mr. Matthews talked to the probation officer that was in charge and introduced him to Sam. "Sam, this is Arthur, Arthur Taylor." "Nice to meet you Mr. Taylor." "Same here." The three of them then went over the rules of the house to let Sam know what would be expected and what was not allowed. Mr. Matthews took off for the evening. "Remember Sam, just give me a call if you need anything." "Thanks Mr. Matthews." Mr. Taylor then took Sam upstairs and led him to his room. It wasn't the best but it sure beat his prison cell. "This is your room Sam. You'll have to share the bathroom with the other residents of this floor. There is a bathroom at each end of the hallway. If you need anything just come downstairs. I'll be there." "Thanks Mr. Taylor." Sam sat on the bed and took in his new surroundings. He fell back on the bed and looked at the ceiling and began reflect on the day's events. He hadn't been free for 24 hours, yet it felt as if it had been 24 years. "I never realized what being locked up could do to you" thought Sam. He had been incarcerated for only three years but it seemed an eternity. He once again had his freedom, but his prospects for jobs were minimal if not outright nonexistent. Sam felt that he could get something to get back on his feet to get re-established, he just didn't know what. "I guess this is where my faith is really going to be tested" he thought. After lying on the bed contemplating his next move, Sam got up and took a shower and called it a night.

Chapter 16

Dawn of a New Day

Sam awoke to the annoying sound of a car alarm blaring through his new neighborhood. His first night as a free man had gone pretty uneventfully. The halfway house was quiet as rules were strictly enforced regarding noise levels. He didn't have a television of his own and the one in the lounge area usually was pretty much spoken for. The wait for bathroom time was not as bad as he had expected. "This isn't so bad after all" thought Sam. He went downstairs and asked Mr. Taylor if he could use a phone. "Pay phone is on the wall in the lounge. My phone is to be used only for emergencies and calls to your probation officer" he explained. "I understand. I need to call Mr. Matthews." "Go ahead then." Sam dialed Mr. Matthews office and got no answer. He tried a second time to no avail. He then dialed the main number. Finally, success. "Is Mr. Matthews in?" "No, he is in court this morning. He probably won't be in until about 1:00. May I take a message?" "Tell him Sam Banks called." "I'll let him know." Sam wondered what his next move would be. He asked Mr. Taylor if there was somewhere close by that he could get some breakfast. "There's a diner two blocks away from here. Can't miss it."

Sam went off to get some breakfast. He walked slowly so he could appreciate every second of this moment. "Sure feels good to be able to walk without being told where to go and when to stop." It had been three years since he had been able to take a walk on his own or go without being told where it was he was going or when to come back from where he was headed. Sam longed for this moment and now he was reveling in it.

He leisurely strolled along until he arrived at the diner. Upon entering, he saw a young waitress that was incredible. "She is quite possibly the most beautiful woman I've ever seen!" thought Sam. I'm going to make sure I sit in her area. He noticed the area that she was serving and found an empty table. Noticing Sam sitting at the table she came over to ask if he would be dining alone. "Yes, just me. I'd like some black coffee please." "Sure, coming right up." Sam was really impressed after seeing her up close. "She is gorgeous. I don't want to seem too aggressive so I'll play it cool." The waitress came back with the coffee and asked Sam if he was ready to place his order. "Yes I am" he replied. He then gave his order and began to drink his coffee. While he waited on his food he watched her every move. A few minutes passed and she brought Sam his food. "Will there be anything else?" "Well, could you tell me your name if I do need something?" "Sheila, my name is Sheila. Just call me if you need anything." "Sheila, that's a pretty name…for a pretty woman." "Thank you." "You're welcome." Sam really didn't eat his food as he continued to train his eyes on Sheila during the whole time he was there. She came by and asked him occasionally if he wanted or needed something. Then finally, she noticed he had barely touched his food. "You weren't hungry at all were you?" "Not really" answered Sam. "Well, why did you order something if you didn't plan on eating?" "Well I was hungry, until I saw you. I guess you can say you took my breath and my appetite away." Sheila didn't know how to respond. She being an attractive woman had been hit on numerous times by guys trying to come on to her. But something seemed different about this time. "What is your name?" "Sam Banks." "I haven't seen you around here before, you new to the neighborhood?" "I'll be honest with you. I live in a halfway house a few blocks from here. I just got out of prison yesterday."

"Prison, goodbye!" "No, wait. What I did was terrible, but I'm not a monster or anything like that. I was drunk one night leaving a club and I was in an accident and a man was killed." "Are you serious?" "Yes. I did three years because I was fortunate enough to get a plea bargain. I've accepted Jesus Christ as my Lord and Savior and I have realized the error of my ways. Please, won't you talk to me?" Sheila sat down and the two of them began to talk. She then realized that she was supposed to be working. "What time do you get off?" "Three o'clock. Then I have to go to class. I attend school in the evenings." "Can I have your phone number?" Sam asked nervously. "I guess so." Sam took the number and went back to the halfway house to wait until he could get in touch with Mr. Matthews.

Back in his room, Sam thought about what to do to pass the time. He wanted to get in touch with Tim, but wasn't quite sure what kind of response he would get. "I've been out of prison a day and a half. I really should get in touch with Tim" thought Sam. He went to the lounge and dialed Tim's work number. There was no answer. He then tried Tim at home. Again, no answer. He then tried a cell phone number he had for Tim. Finally, success. "What's up man, where are you" asked Sam. "Who's this?" replied Tim. "This is Sam, don't you recognize my voice?" "Oh yeah. How's it going Sam. You got out yesterday didn't you?" "I sure did. I'm at the halfway house I'm staying in for the next couple of weeks. You didn't go to work today?" "No, had some business to take care of. How are things going for you?" "Well, it's strange being back out but I won't complain because God is too good for that." "There you go again with that God talk." "Tim, I know you're not an atheist. Why do you try to cut me off whenever I mention God?" "We've been through this before and I don't want to go down that road again, but you know how I feel." "And you know my feelings as well." "If that's what you called for you shouldn't have wasted your time." "I'll keep you in my prayers Tim." "Whatever dog, peace." That would be the last time Sam talked to Tim.

Sam began to get nervous as 3:00 approached and he had yet to hear back from Mr. Matthews. He hadn't thought to ask him for his pager number and Mr. Matthews didn't bother to provide it. While he wasn't required to get in touch with him everyday, Sam desperately wanted to start the process of finding a job and getting back on his feet. Growing tired of striking out he quit trying to call Mr. Matthews and began to think about his new friend Sheila he had met at the diner. "I wonder what time she gets home. How could I forget to ask that important question" Sam wondered. He tried to call Sheila to no avail as her phone continued to ring with no answer. "Just wasn't meant for me to talk to anyone today." "You haven't talked to me Sam." "God is that you." "Yes it is. Don't put me on the backburner now that you're out of prison Sam. As you get things in order in your life it is I who will be the one who orchestrates how things should and should not go. Don't forget Sam." "I hear you God."

Chapter 17

Anxiety

The next day Sam woke up bright and early with his day already planned out. First he was going to the diner to eat breakfast – and see Sheila. Next he was going to get a newspaper to continue his job search. Lastly he was going to make it a point to get in touch with Mr. Matthews. After getting dressed he rushed out of the house on his way to the diner. Sam hurriedly went hoping to see Sheila. After looking around and not seeing her, he asked one of the other waitresses if she was at work. "She's off today." "Thank you" sighed Sam. He was disappointed that he hadn't been able to get in touch with her now he wouldn't see her either. Dejectedly he left the diner. Seeing a newspaper stand, he bought a paper and went back to his room to target potential job opportunities. After that he went to call Mr. Matthews. Finally he was able to get him. "Mr. Matthews, Sam Banks here." "How are you Banks, you didn't need to get in touch with me again until next week." "I know, just wanted to touch bases with you." "Everything alright Banks?" "Yes, things just seem to be slow going." "Banks you just got out less than 48 hours ago. Give it time, you'll start to see some wheels turning. I must say I like your attitude. Keep your head up." "I will Mr. Matthews." Sam then remembered God reminding him not to leave Him out of his life. He picked his Bible up and read some scriptures. Having read it so often while he was in prison, it was as if his Bible just fell open to Hebrews 11:1: *Now faith is the substance of things hoped for, the evidence of things not seen.* As always, God showed him the appropriate message for his situation at the appropriate time. "Thank you again God. I just can't put into words how glad I am that you're in my life."

Nightfall approached and Sam decided to give Sheila a call. He went down to the lounge only to find the phone in use. Waiting for what seemed like forever, the phone was finally free. Sam anxiously dialed the numbers. After two rings, there was an answer. "Hello." "Sheila, is that you?" "Yes, who's calling?" "This is Sam Banks. We met at the diner you work in on yesterday." "Oh yes, I remember now. How are you." "Fine. I went there looking for you today." "I'm off on Wednesdays and Sundays." "I see. Did I disturb you?" "Well I was studying for a big test I have coming up on Friday." "Oh yeah, what are you studying?" "I'm studying biology." "What's your major?" "Science. I'm planning on going to medical school." "That's interesting." "I'd like to continue to chat, but I really need to get in these books." "I understand, I've been there. Will you be at work tomorrow, I'd like to see you." "Yes. I'll be there." "Good, I'll see you then."

Sam felt better than he did earlier. He'd really like to have seen Sheila, but talking to her would have to suffice until tomorrow. Again he turned his attention to the newspaper to look at job openings he would target. Before being released from prison, Sam had sent out close to 200 résumés and only three companies even decided to write him a rejection letter acknowledging receipt of his résumé. Not getting a response let him know what they thought. "It's going to be almost impossible for me to get a job with this felony on my record. Why was I so stupid that night." Beginning to feel sorry for himself, he found solace as he had many times before in the Word of God. He picked up his Bible and found a scripture that was more than fitting for his situation where Jesus says '*the things which are impossible with men are possible with God.* [46]' After reading Sam said to himself

"No matter how hopeless my situation looks, I know that God can give me the favor I need in spite of my record. And I trust Him to give me the job He wants me to have."

Morning came and Sam had a renewed outlook on things. He was going to try a different approach to his job search. Rather than looking solely at engineering firms, he decided to approach schools to inquire about teaching, after all he had a degree in mathematics. He prepared résumés and sent them to various colleges and universities. Once again he received letters of recommendation from the counselor at the prison and some of the ministers who came to preach at the chapel during his incarceration. "Surely, something will come through for me in this area" Sam reasoned.

Sam continued to type cover letters to submit with his résumés and before he realized it, the day had gotten away from him. It was now 2:30. "I'm going to miss Sheila!" Sam hurriedly got dressed and ran the two blocks to Sheila's diner to get there before her shift ended at 3:00. Just as he was entering the door, she was getting her belongings. "I almost missed you. Wouldn't have wanted to go two days without seeing you" said Sam. "Well, you made it just in time didn't you, but I'm on my way to school now" replied Sheila. "Can I at least escort you there?" asked Sam. "I don't see why not." The subway station was about a block away. Just as they began to leave the diner, the two of them felt rain drops. "On no" thought Sheila. "I don't have an umbrella, do you?" "Nope" replied Sam. "Let's make a run for it." Sam took Sheila's books and grabbed her by the hand and the two of them took off. Just as the rain picked up, the subway station was in their sights. "We can beat the heavy rain, we're right here" shouted Sam. The very moment that the heavens opened up they stepped inside the subway station. "Boy, we just made it" said Sam. "You didn't get too wet did you?" he asked. "No, I'm fine. I should be okay." They tried to get on the first train that arrived, but it was filled. "Let's let this one pass. My class doesn't start until 4:15" said Sheila. "That's fine with me" replied Sam. Another train came and it had a little room so they decided to get onboard. Sam shared with Sheila his new approach regarding his job search. "Are you having a hard time finding something given your situation?" she asked. "Yes, but I'm keeping my head up. The Bible says that *'my God shall supply all your need according to his riches in glory by Christ Jesus.⁴⁷'* I have to remind myself of that whenever I get discouraged." "So, you read the Bible?" Sheila asked. "Yes I do. I am a Christian." "Forgive me if I sound sarcastic, but don't most guys that go to prison suddenly find God?" "I know where you're going and yes that does happen. But like I briefly told you when we first met, after the accident God spoke to me while I was hospitalized because I needed rest and He offered me rest. When I did go to prison I recognized I needed Him in my life and I accepted Jesus Christ as my Lord and Savior. Only after doing that was I able to cope with things that I had to face and I am able to have a positive outlook in spite of how things appear." "You sound like you mean that." "I do Sheila. Without Jesus I would have probably gone insane in prison. But because of Him I have *'the peace of God that surpasseth all understanding.⁴⁸'*"

After three stops they were at Sheila's school. A large number of the people emptied off the train at this particular stop. Sam got off and walked Sheila to the building her class was in. "What time do your classes end for the night?" "My last class ends at 8:00." "Do you usually go home alone?" "There are a couple of other girls in my class that ride the train with me and sometimes I get a ride, it just depends." "Can I come and meet you sometimes?" asked Sam. "Sure you can." "How about tonight?" "I guess that will be okay." Sam walked around the campus for a little while reminiscing on his own college days. He saw the sights of campus life and then he had an idea. "Why don't I see if they have any opportunities available here?" Sam went to find the human resources department. After getting lost, he stopped and asked for directions. "It's in the building right across the street on the third floor." He went into the building and found that they were just about to close for the day. Sam pleaded with the lady at the front counter to hear him out. He explained his situation, laying all of his cards on the table. The woman listened intently and told Sam that she would refer him to her supervisor. "Thank you for at least hearing me out." Sam took the business card she offered and went on his way.

Sam went to get a bite to eat and watch television. Impatiently he watched the clock tick slowly as he longed for 8:00 to arrive. "Time is going by too slow. I can't wait to see Sheila" he thought. Finally it was 7:30. Sam left to walk back to meet Sheila. As he arrived at her class, she was coming out of the door with some friends. "Got here just in time I see." "Yes, you've got perfect timing." Sheila then introduced Sam to her friends and excused herself from them to join Sam. The two of them walked back to the subway station. Upon arriving there it dawned on Sam that he didn't know where Sheila lived. He wanted to see her home but had to keep in mind he needed to get back to the halfway house by 10:00 for curfew. "I'd like to see you home, but I have to get back by 10:00. Where do you live anyway?" "I live in College Park, it's not too far but you'd probably better not risk getting yourself in any trouble." "You're right. I can stay out until 11:00 on the weekends, how about we get together then." "Sure, I'm free this Saturday." "Good, but I'll come to the diner to see you between now and then." Sam went back to the halfway house feeling pretty good about himself. He had met a nice young lady and his job search was going to take a change for the better he thought. "God things are really looking up. Thank you."

Chapter 18

Sam's Fall

Sam called the gentleman that he was referred to by the human resources department at Sheila's school. His name was Don Thomas. "Hi Mr. Thomas, this is Sam Banks. I was given your card by the receptionist at the human resources department." "Yes, she told me to expect your call, how may I help you?" "I was wondering if I could talk with you. I'm looking for work. I didn't have a résumé with me at the time, but I have to be up front and tell you that I just got out of prison." "I see." "I was charged with vehicular homicide and served three years. During my incarceration I was eligible for early parole and received a number of recommendations from counselors and ministers. All that I need is a chance and I hope and pray that you will provide one or help me in some way." "I admire your honesty and openness Sam. While I don't have any openings at the present time, I will make some phone calls to see what I can do to help you. You appear to be a conscientious young man who has put his past mistakes behind him." "I have Mr. Thomas. I am clean and sober now and I have a renewed outlook on life. I was an engineer but I'd like to get into teaching." "Give me a few days and get back in touch with me to see what I could find out." "Thanks for hearing me out and I appreciate whatever you do." "My pleasure Sam."

After talking with Mr. Thomas, Sam got dressed and went to the diner to have breakfast – but more importantly to see Sheila. He walked in and saw that it was extremely busy this particular morning. Sheila's station was filled, so he would have to sit at the counter. Sheila saw Sam and came over to greet him. "Good morning, how are you?" "Fine, you look good as always." "Thanks. That table will be clear in a minute or two. Why don't you come sit over there once they leave." "I'll do that." Sheila cleared the table after her customers left and Sam immediately went over to sit down. "Will you have your usual?" Sheila asked. "You know me" replied Sam. Just as he was finishing his breakfast, Sheila sat down for a minute. Sam told her about his conversation with Mr. Thomas. "That sounds great. I hope he finds something that you really like." "Well, this is new for me. I've never taught but I know that I can do it." "I'm sure you can do anything you put your mind to Sam."

Saturday arrived and none too soon. Sam had really enjoyed talking with Sheila and was beginning to fall for her fast. "I sure didn't expect to meet someone as nice and gorgeous as Sheila my first week out, but I'm glad that I did" thought Sam. On his way to the subway station he stopped by a sidewalk vendor and purchased a single rose to present to her. Upon arriving at the subway station he was greeted by an announcement over the PA system: "Due to a malfunctioning rail car, we are experiencing delays in our service. Please be patient and we apologize for any inconvenience." "This is just great" sighed Sam. He had waited all week and now he was being delayed from his big moment. "Nothing I can do but wait, so it's no need to get upset" thought Sam. About 20 minutes passed and finally a train arrived. Due to the delay it was filled with passengers. Sam saw this but he wasn't about to let that stop him. He squeezed in and boarded the train. "Please hurry up and get to her stop" he thought. People slowly filed out at each station until there was finally some breathing room. Sheila's stop was the end of the line and they didn't arrive a moment too soon as he was about to burst with anticipation.

Sam arrived at Sheila's apartment. When she opened the door to greet him Sam was blown away. "You look amazing!" he said. "Thank you. I wanted to look my best" answered Sheila. "You succeeded" replied Sam. She invited him in and began to get her belongings. Sam asked Sheila to close her eyes so that he could give her the rose. "This is for you." "That was so sweet of you!" she replied. She gave him a kiss on the cheek. "If I had known to expect that I would have gotten you a whole dozen" replied Sam. "You're so silly. Where are we going?" asked Sheila. "Seeing as how I haven't done this in the past three years, I thought we'd do something I haven't been able to do: go to a movie." "That sounds fine." The two of them left to go to the movie theater. After the movie they went to grab a bite to eat. It seemed as if the time had zoomed by for it was now 9:00. Sam had to be in by 11:00 but he wanted to see Sheila home safely before going himself. He decided he could pull off doing both so he took Sheila home. Upon arriving at her apartment, Sheila asked "Can't you stay for just a minute?" "That's as long as I can stay." Sam went in and Sheila offered him something to drink. "No thanks, I'm fine." The two of them began to talk and Sheila asked "How long have you been going to church?" "Not long. I accepted Christ as my Lord and Savior in the hospital after my accident. How about you?" "Well to be honest, I went to church when I was growing up, but since I've been on my own and in school I haven't had much time to go. Sundays I usually catch up on my studying and run errands and do chores around the house." "I was planning to find a church in my neighborhood to go to on tomorrow, would you like to go with me?" asked Sam. "As I said, I study on Sundays and I have a million things to do before Monday, so I'll have to pass" answered Sheila. "Maybe I could help you study and run errands, etc." offered Sam. "I'd like that. What time could you be here?" "Whatever is convenient for you." "I'll be here at noon." "Sounds good." Off Sam went. After leaving Sheila's apartment, he realized how quickly he had put off going to church to go and help Sheila. "Oh well" he thought. "Missing one Sunday won't kill me."

The next day Sam went over to see Sheila as planned. While she studied, he went to the laundry room in her complex and began her laundry. He began to read a magazine after putting detergent into the machines. As he began reading an article he heard a voice. "Sam." He looked around but saw that no one else was in the laundry room besides him. Again, he heard a voice. "Sam." "Who's that?" asked Sam. "Sam, you know my voice." "God, is that you?" "Yes Sam. Why did you choose to forgo church today?" "I'm helping out a friend." "Sam, you must not get comfortable and leave me out of your life. Not only did you need me while you were in prison, you will need me now and always." "I know God and I understand." *"Behold I stand at the door and knock, if any man hear my voice and open the door I will come in to him and will sup with him and he with me.[49]'* Remember Sam, you must seek Me for *I am a rewarder of them that diligently seek me.[50]"*

Sam finished Sheila's laundry and went back to the apartment. Exhausted from school and work, Sheila had fallen asleep while studying. Sam woke her up to let her know that he was back. "I must have dozed off" she said. "Yes you did. Should I leave so that you can get some sleep." "No, don't go yet. I made dinner for you." "You didn't have to do that." "I wanted to. You've been so nice to me. Most guys that I've met since I started school have all been about one thing and you have been the total opposite. Even after you told me about your prison sentence and all I didn't feel uncomfortable deciding to see you." "Well, that's great to know. I can't lie you're a very attractive woman but I respect you."

Sheila served Sam dinner consisting of tossed salad, steak, baked potatoes, and mixed vegetables. "Would you like any dessert?" she asked. "No, I'm stuffed. That was delicious. Who taught you how to cook?" "My grandmother did. She raised me." "Is that so." "Yes. My parents got a divorce when I was young and my mother didn't really do a good job of taking care of me so my grandmother took me in." "My father walked out on my mother but she did the best she could to raise me and my two sisters." "That's why you're so sensitive and sweet. You were raised in a house full of women." "If you say so." The evening went on and the two of them continued to talk. It was getting late and Sam needed to get back to the halfway house. "I sure hate to leave but I have to go." "I hate to see you leave." As she walked Sam to the door, Sam turned around and the two of them embraced. Sam said "I'd better let go of you before something happens." "Nothing will happen that neither of us doesn't want to happen" replied Sheila. The two of them kissed and went back inside. Before long, they had gone Sheila's bedroom and were intimate with one another.

Sam looked at the clock. It was 10:30. "What will I do, I'll get in trouble if I'm late!" "Wait, I can ask my neighbor to give you a ride." Sheila gave her neighbor a call who just happened to be walking in the door. She asked him to give Sam a ride and he agreed. Sam hurriedly got dressed and told Sheila he would come to see her on tomorrow. "We have a lot to discuss" he said. "I know. I'll see you then."

Chapter 19

Breakthrough

Getting a ride was exactly what the doctor ordered. Sam made it back to the halfway house with no time to spare. "How can I ever repay you?" Sam asked Sheila's neighbor. "No problem man, glad I could help out." Sam rushed inside to barely make curfew. "You're pushing it Banks" Mr. Taylor smirked. "I'm here. That's all that matters" replied Sam. Sam walked to his room slowly. He had worked so hard to get back before curfew what he had done hadn't had time to sink in. Upon getting to his room he plopped down on the bed. "Why did I just do that? I know I wanted to but I shouldn't have done it" he thought. "What is she going to think of me now?" Sam had all sorts of thoughts running through his mind. He knew he was wrong and needed to ask for forgiveness, but he didn't feel like he could. "I've messed up too bad. God won't forgive me for that. I knew better." After anguishing over what happened, he finally went to sleep.

Morning came and Sam called Mr. Thomas. It had been a couple of days since they last spoke and Sam wanted to see if he had been able to find him anything. "Hello, Mr. Thomas?" "Speaking." "This is Sam Banks. We talked last week." "Oh yes, Sam how are you?" "Fine. I was just checking to see if you had any news for me." "Well, I called as many of my contacts as I could. The only thing I could come up with may or may not interest you, but you could use it as a stepping stone to something else." "What is it?" "Well this community college is willing to give you a chance as a part time math teacher. Being part time you wouldn't get benefits and the pay isn't great but it's a start." "I know I have to crawl before I can walk. Give me the information." Sam took the information and went to see Mr. Matthews as he was required to. "How's it going Banks?" "Good. I've got a lead on a job." "Already. I told you that the wheels would start turning but I didn't think they'd turn this fast." "Well, I don't want to sit around not doing anything. I'm ready to get going." "Where exactly is this job you've found?" Sam went on to tell Mr. Matthews about the opportunity and how it came about. "Sounds like a good opportunity. I hope it works out."

Sam left Mr. Matthews office and headed for the school. He went to the human resources department and told them who he was and who referred him. After a brief wait, the human resources director came to greet Sam. "Sam Banks." "Yes, I'm Sam Banks." "Good morning. Dan told me about you. I'm Jim Phillips." "Nice to meet you Mr. Phillips." "Call me Jim." "I'm aware of your past Sam and Dan told me that I should give you a chance." "Yes sir, I do have a record but I have more than learned from the error of my ways." "I see. Why do you want to teach?" "I was an engineer before my incarceration, but I haven't found any open doors upon my release. As a result I thought that it was probably best for me to go in a new direction professionally as well as personally." "Well Sam, you seem to be more than adequately qualified for the position. Seeing that you haven't taught before, I want to start you off slowly. This gives you a chance to check out whether or not this is for you and we will have the opportunity to see if this will work from our perspective." "I understand." "Our school caters to students who are continuing their studies or those who stopped them and are getting back on track. Because of this we have a high demand for night and weekend classes. You would be required to teach two weekends out of the month. Will this pose a problem for you?" "No. I'm grateful for the opportunity and I want to make the most of it. I do have one question though." "What is it Sam?" "Could this lead to a full time opportunity if everything works out?" "If all sides agree I don't see why not. Here's my card. Give me a call in a few days and we'll finalize everything and you can start later this week." "Sounds good to me."

Sam left the school feeling like a million bucks. He was getting his shot he desperately needed and wanted as well. Sam couldn't wait to get to the diner to see Sheila and tell her the good news. He hopped on the train and went directly to the diner. Upon entering he looked around, but didn't see her. "Where's Sheila?" he asked another waitress. "She called in sick today." "Thanks." Sam left to go back to his room. "I hope she's alright" he thought. With his mind beginning to wander about Sheila he hurried back to the house. Surprisingly the phone was free. He dialed the phone as fast as he could to call Sheila. "Hello, Sheila." "Yes Sam." "How are you. I just came from the diner and saw that you weren't there. Is everything alright?" "Well yes and no. I feel bad about what happened last night. You seemed to me to be sincere about being a Christian and, well you know the rest." "Sheila, if there is anyone to blame it should be me. I am more than attracted to you but I let my flesh get the best of me. I hope you don't take me for one of those guys that you had been meeting." "No, that's just the thing and I hope you don't think bad about me." "Of course not. Can I come over to see you?" "Well I'm going to class in a little while. I just didn't feel like being around anyone this morning." "I understand. I'll call you later tonight."

Sam really felt bad now. He liked Sheila but he didn't want to hurt her. Now that this had happened he didn't know how to approach things. One thing was certain, he didn't intend on putting her out of his life. Sam was determined to make things right and try to do all he could to make their relationship work.

Chapter 20

Losing Touch

Friday arrived and just as Mr. Phillips had promised Sam was able to start his teaching position. Sam arrived at school promptly at 12:00. His first class was to begin at 3:00. "Glad to have you aboard Sam." "Glad to be here." Mr. Phillips took Sam around and introduced him to a few of the other teachers. Being that it was a small school there was a 'hometown' feel to it. Sam completed some paperwork and then went to talk to Mr. Phillips. "Don't be nervous Sam. I know you've never taught before but your students won't know unless you tell them. Just be calm and share your knowledge and everything will work out fine." "Thanks Mr. Phillips. I'm so nervous." "You're going to be alright." He escorted Sam to his classroom to allow him some time to himself before getting started. In the previous 3+ years Sam had grown accustomed to praying and/or reading scriptures before taking on a new task. However Sam had begun to subtly neglect the things he had done. He hadn't gone to church since his release, he barely read his Bible and he couldn't remember the last time he prayed. Sam embarked upon his teaching career like he previously did things in his life – on his own.

Sam taught two classes on his first day and things went pretty well considering it was a new career. "I think I'm going to like teaching" thought Sam. Mr. Phillips came by afterwards to see how things went. "Well Sam, what do you think?" "This is definitely going to work." "Good. You seemed to have made a good first impression with the students, that's always important." "Don't I know it." Sam went to the office to drop off some paperwork and to his surprise Sheila was waiting on him. "I decided to come and see how your first day went." "It was great. It's even better now that I see you." "I'm glad to hear that." The two of them left and went back to Sheila's apartment. She made Sam a celebration dinner in honor of his first day. She even bought him a cake to commemorate the occasion. "You didn't have to do all of this." "I know, but I wanted to." After dinner the two of them began to watch a movie. Sam realizing his curfew was drawing nigh decided it was time to call it a night. "As much as I want to stay, I'd better get going." "I'll be glad when you are out of that place." "You and me both." "Where are you going to stay when you leave the halfway house?" "My probation officer is supposed to help me find a place I guess. I hadn't really thought about it. I have to stay there another month you know." "Well, you can stay with me" said Sheila. "Are you serious?" "Yes. I have the room. I'm here all alone and we are getting serious." "This is true." "Just think about it. I'm not pressuring you or anything, just making an offer." "I'll definitely think about it."

Sam went home and Sheila's offer was all he could think about. "Man, I can't believe she asked me to move in with her. As much as I'd like to, I don't know if I should make a move like that so soon." Sam got to the halfway house and asked Mr. Taylor what would happen when his time was up there. "Well, you've got to find a place of your own." "Does Mr. Matthews help me or is it something I have to do?" he asked. "Sometimes the probation officer's help you out but normally you find it yourself. You'd be better off talking to him." "I will."

Two weeks passed and Sam was getting comfortable in his new profession. "I should have been a teacher all along" thought Sam. Things were going great at school and even better between he and Sheila. They didn't go two days without seeing one another. He was becoming a fixture at her apartment and all of her coworkers at the diner knew him.

Early Monday morning Sam got up to go and check in with Mr. Matthews. "I could tell from your file and evaluations that I was getting a model citizen in you Banks" said Mr. Matthews. "Thanks." "How are things going on your new job?" "Everything is fine. I do have one question. I'm less than two weeks away from my time being up at the house, do you help me find a place or should I be looking on my own?" "Well generally we'd like for you to go with a relative. Since you don't have any family here I could help you find a place or have you been able to find something?" "Well I have a prospect that looks good but I just wanted to check with you first." "Is that so." "Yes sir." "If it's a sure thing, then go for it. One thing, you must have a phone so that I can contact you." "I will, that will be no problem." "Looks like to me you've got it all planned out." "Looks that way doesn't it." Now Sam had the go ahead to do what he wanted to do but knew he shouldn't do – he was going to move in with Sheila.

After leaving Mr. Matthews' office, Sam checked his watch to see if he could make a quick stop by the diner to see Sheila before going to work. "I think I can pull it off" he reasoned. He rushed to the subway station and hopped on the train to see her. He arrived at the diner and saw her the moment he walked in. As usual he went to sit in her station and she came over with water and his now infamous black coffee. "Good morning Sam. How did your meeting go with Mr. Matthews?" "Everything went fine. You remember that proposal you offered?" "About moving in with me?" "Yes." "Is it still available?" "Definitely!" "Well, I intend to take you up on it as soon as I get out of the house." Sheila put her tray down and hugged Sam. "I'm so happy. I'm glad I met you Sam Banks." "No, I'm even happier that I met you Sheila."

Sam left the diner with mixed emotions. Even though he had been inching away from God ever since his release, the seed of God's Word was planted in his heart. He knew that God is a holy God and that He doesn't honor any "arrangements" between man and woman besides marriage. However, Sam had convinced himself that this was in his best interest to move in with Sheila. "Where else do I have to go?" he thought. Knowing that he had been constantly reminded about trusting in God during his incarceration only made Sam feel even more self-conscious of the decision he had just made. In spite of it all, he chose to follow through as planned and move in with Sheila.

Two weeks passed and Sam's time at the halfway house had come to an end. "Except for that one night you were almost late Banks, I can't say that I had any trouble out of you. I wish all of the residents were like you" said Mr. Taylor. "Well I didn't want any trouble and I'm glad to be leaving." Sam gathered his belongings and hurriedly exited the halfway house. Sheila was waiting downstairs. She had borrowed her neighbor's car so that they wouldn't have to take the subway. "I'm glad this day has finally arrived" said Sheila. "You and me both" he replied. "Things are going to work out fine" she answered.

Shortly after arriving at their home, Sam remembered he had to check in with Mr. Matthews. "I need to call my probation officer." "I meant to tell you Sam, my phone was disconnected." "What did you say?" "Things were a little tight and I had to sacrifice something and that seemed the most logical – especially now that I would be living with you and not have to worry about how I could get in touch with you." "What am I supposed to do now. I need to have a phone available to get in touch with Mr. Matthews and I gave him this number." "Well, can't you pay it?" "Looks like I'll have to. I need to call him before I go to work." Sam stormed out of the house to find a pay phone to call Mr. Matthews. After walking a block or so he saw a pay phone. "Mr. Matthews?" "Speaking." "Sam Banks here." "Banks, I tried the number you gave me and it was disconnected. You know the rules." "I know, I'm not trying to do anything underhanded. Things just got off track little bit. The service should be restored tomorrow at the latest." "Alright Banks. How's the job coming along?" "Fine. I'm off to work as soon as I hang up with you. Didn't want to get on your bad side so I knew to call you." "Well you did the right thing. Make sure you get that phone back on like you promised." "I will Mr. Matthews." Sam hung up and went to work. His day had started out wonderfully, but now he was faced with the pressure of getting the phone service restored – and fast. "Why didn't she tell me this earlier" he thought. "Can't cry over spilled milk now. Just have to get it taken care of." Sam went to school, but he couldn't get his mind off of the disconnected phone. After classes were over he rushed home. Sheila had yet to arrive from her classes. He waited impatiently for her to arrive. The moment she walked in the door he asked her: "Just how much is the phone bill?" "Well good evening to you" replied Sheila sarcastically. "I'm sorry, it's just that I have to have a phone to satisfy my probation." "I know and I hate I had to let it get disconnected." "Please just tell me how much it is" he pleaded. "Two hundred dollars" she answered. "You've got to be kidding. Why so much?" "There is a past due balance and a fee to restore the service. I have some of it but not all." "That's all I've managed to save" replied Sam, "but I've got to have a phone so here goes." Sam reluctantly gave Sheila the money to pay the bill. "Thank you. Now that there are two incomes, this shouldn't happen again." "I sure hope not."

Chapter 21

Drama

About a month passed and Sam decided that he and Sheila needed to sit down and work out a budget. After grading papers he wrote some ideas down and prepared them to present to her when she arrived from school. When he finished, Sam started watching a movie. To his surprise, Sheila came in almost two hours earlier than usual. "Why aren't you in class?" he asked. "I hadn't been feeling well so I went to the doctor today. Sam, I'm pregnant." "What did you just say?" asked Sam. "I said I'm pregnant" replied Sheila. "You can't be, I mean, this just isn't happening." "It is Sam. I'm six weeks pregnant." Sam was now in deeper than he ever planned or thought he would be. His moment of weakness had now come back for him to face. "What am I going to do with a baby?" he thought. "Neither of us is ready to handle this. I guess I should have thought about that before." Suddenly Sam got up and grabbed his jacket. "I need some fresh air." "Wait Sam, don't leave. Let's talk about this" pleaded Sheila. "I'll be back. I've got to go and clear my head." Sam left and took a long walk. He thought about his life from his own childhood when his father left, his struggles during college, and his engineering career. Everything he saw was done his way. All that he had were miserable memories of frustration and unhappiness. The only period he could see something that didn't have "Sam Banks" written all over it was when he was in prison and he had come to know Jesus as his Lord and Savior. Now, instead of drawing closer to Him, Sam had chosen to move away from Him. "What a mess I've made of things. Sheila isn't ready to be a mother and I'm not ready to be a father. On top of that, we're not married."

Sam returned about an hour later. Sheila had been crying and waiting for him to return. "Why didn't you stay and talk to me like I asked you to?" she asked. "I needed to clear my head." "Are you going to have to clear your head when the baby gets here?" "What's that supposed to mean?" "I mean are you going to walk away or can I count on you to be in this with me." "Of course I'm going to be here. The suddenness of the moment just over-whelmed me. Things are going to work out fine." "I really needed to hear that." They held each other and pondered over their future and what awaited them. Sam said to Sheila "I'll be honest with you, I'm not ready to be a father but I don't have much of a choice now." "Same with me, but we'll make it together."

Morning came and Sam got up early to prepare breakfast for Sheila. "I think I'll surprise her, she's had a long night" he thought. He cooked eggs, bacon and toast. Sheila smelled the aroma and got up to see where it was coming from. "Surprise!" shouted Sam. "What's going on?" "I just wanted to do something special for a special person." "Why thank you. How sweet of you. That's what attracted me to you. You are so sweet." "I hope you enjoy it." "I'm sure I will it smells great." After eating break-fast, Sam cleaned up the dishes and got dressed. "I'm going to go to talk to Jim and see if he will give me a full time position." "That sounds like a good idea. How long did he initially say you would have to wait before being considered for a full time posi-tion?" "He didn't say really. Just that we would see how things worked out. Now that you're pregnant, I have to get full time work with benefits because you won't be working anymore." "Why do you think I won't be working?" "Because, I don't want my child's mother working – especially in a diner on your feet all day." "Don't you think I have a right to decide whether or not I quit working?" "Sheila, I'm not going to argue with you about this. You are going to quit your job!" The two of them engaged in a shouting match over the issue of Sheila working. Finally Sam shouted "I'm not saying anything else. I'm going to work and you're going to quit your job and that is final!" Sam stormed out of the apartment on his way to the subway station. "I can't believe her. Here it is she has a good man that wants to provide for her and their child and she is acting this way. Why won't she just cooperate."

Sam arrived at the school at 11:00. When Mr. Phillips saw him, he was caught off guard. "Sam, why are you here so early?" "I need to talk to you." "Is everything okay?" "Well, yes and no. You see, I need to know if I can be considered for a full time position." "I do believe we spoke about the possibility of that." "How soon can it become a reality. I really need a full time job." "Well Sam, I'll have to speak with my boss and go from there. You've been doing a good job and your students seem satisfied. I'll let you know what I find out." Sam left the office feeling pretty good about his chances of getting a full time position.

After class was done Sam packed up and got ready for the confrontation that certainly awaited when he got home. As a peace offering he stopped off to buy Sheila a dozen roses and a teddy bear. When he arrived home Sheila was nowhere in sight. He went to a neighbor's that Sheila visited on occasion to see if she was there to no avail. He went back to the apartment to wait. "This isn't like her. She would call me or leave a note if she's going to be late." Trying to get his mind off of the fact she was not there, Sam started grading some of his students' tests. He dozed off about halfway through them. Suddenly he was awakened by the sound of the door opening. "Sheila, is that you." "Yes." "Where have you been?" "I needed to vent so I went with Pam to talk after class." "I see. Are you still upset with me?" "Yes and no. You didn't give me a chance to give my feelings about working before you decided for me that I should quit. I got so angry. I must say however, that I do appreciate the fact that you want to take care of things. You must understand. I've been on my own every since I was 18 and it's hard for someone so independent to give that up." "Believe me I understand. It's just that I couldn't bear the thought of something happening to you if were working somewhere. I'd rather have the peace of mind of knowing that you were resting and able to take it easy. Sheila, I love you." "I love you too Sam." They continued to talk and were able to reach a mutual agreement in spite of their differences. Sheila would continue to work until her fifth month of pregnancy.

A week passed by and Sam still hadn't received an answer from Mr. Phillips. "Sheila, I'm leaving now so that I can talk to Mr. Phillips." "Okay, I'll see you tonight." Sam went to the school determined to get some closure to his situation. He arrived at the human resources office and asked for Mr. Phillips. "He's not in yet Sam" the receptionist replied. "When will he get here?" "I'm not sure. He's running late today." Sam sat and waited for about 30 minutes. Finally Mr. Phillips arrived. "Good morning Sam." "Good morning. Mr. Phillips, I need to know if you've found anything out regarding me getting a full time position." "Yes I have Sam. Seeing as how we're in the middle of a semester, we don't have monies budgeted to take on the salary of a full time teacher. We can explore this when the new semester starts. I'll do all I can to see if we can make it happen then." "I really need the benefits Mr. Phillips. Can I qualify for that at least?" "My hands are tied Sam. Policy states that only full time employees are eligible for benefits. I made that clear to you when you accepted the position." "I know, I guess it's not your fault." "Hang in there Sam. Hopefully the new semester will bring better news." Sam left Mr. Phillips' office with other ideas. "I can't wait for him. I'll have to look for another job."

Sam's day ended and not a moment too soon. All he could think about was trying to find a job which would give him some benefits. "I really like it here, but I've got to do what I've got to do." He left and went home to discuss things over with Sheila. "Sheila, I'm going to have to get another job." "But I thought you liked teaching." "I do, but we need the benefits for you and the baby to get proper medical care." "I know, but it seems like we could do something besides you having to quit just when you're beginning to enjoy it." "I know, but there doesn't seem to be any other alternative." Sam had really begun to neglect all of the wonderful things he had learned from walking with God. Not only was he no longer going to church or reading his Bible, his prayer life was totally non-existent and he had even forgotten the one thing that was constantly impressed upon him when he accepted Christ – trusting in Him.

Sam began to look for jobs anywhere he could. He tried to get a job at other small colleges, but to no avail. When he exhausted all of those options Sam then went to look wherever he could. The only job he was able to find that would provide him the benefits he so badly desired was as a night security guard. Sam took the job in spite of Sheila's objections. "When are we going to see each other?" she asked. "We live together don't we?" he replied. "Yes, but when you're home you'll either be asleep or I won't be here and vice versa. I just don't see this working." "Sheila this is not open for debate. You need medical care and this is the way it is going to be and that is final!" Sheila stormed out of the room and began to cry herself to sleep.

Chapter 22

Trouble

Sam resigned from his teaching position and embarked upon his new career as a security guard. He wasn't very comfortable with taking such a position, but felt he had no other choice. The choice to do so would take its toll on his relationship with Sheila as she was concerned with his safety as well as the future of their relationship. As he prepared to leave for his first night on the job Sheila said "I sure hope you come to your senses." "And just what is that supposed to mean?" asked Sam. "You know I don't want you to do such a dangerous job and you're doing it anyway. And to boot we'll hardly ever see each other." "This is just for a short time. I'll keep looking and something is bound to come through." "I just hope you know what you're doing." "Trust me Sheila. I do." Sam gave her a kiss and left the apartment.

Much to his chagrin, Sam's felony conviction prevented him from being able to carry a gun. As such he was given what the security company considered a 'low risk' assignment – he was to monitor an assisted living community. Although in an upscale neighborhood, the facility liked the idea of having someone on the premises. Other than having to make calls for residents who needed medical assistance, there had been no real need for the presence of police or security personnel. "This shouldn't be so bad" Sam thought to himself. "Looks like a piece of cake."

A couple of weeks passed by and Sheila's fears were beginning to come to pass. Sam would come in from his shift just as she was on her way out of the door to go to the diner. One morning as he came in exhausted from work, Sheila said to him "Sam, I don't like what is happening. You are going to have to make a decision. I don't care about benefits. I want you here with me." Sam wanted to erupt but he maintained his cool. "Sheila, we've been through this before. This is how it has to be. Maybe when the new semester starts I can try the school again and see if they will take me back on a full time basis. But for now this is the way things are." "You are so stubborn. I sure hope our child isn't like that." "Sam Banks' child will be just like Sam Banks!" Sheila stormed out of the house and went to work. "I sure wish she would let it go. Doesn't she realize that this is the only way?" thought Sam. "She'll come to the light soon. I know she will."

A month passed and Sam was still doing the security job – against Sheila's desires. Knowing this, he went to his supervisor to ask if there were any daytime assignments he could have. "Banks you know your situation really limits you. All of the prime spots, i.e. daytime positions are filled, and the others require a gun permit which you can't get. This was the only thing I had available where I could use you." "I understand. I was just hoping that maybe something had become available." "If anything does I'll keep you in mind Banks." "Thanks." Sam wanted to make things at home better, but he was having no success finding anything in the daytime with benefits. Things were beginning to get really bad with Sheila as she grew more and more impatient.

Sheila came home from class early one day because she was not feeling well. To her surprise Sam was still in bed. "Shouldn't you be getting dressed for work?" she asked. "My supervisor called. I've been laid off." "You're kidding" she replied. "I'm not happy that you're out of work but at least you won't be doing security." "My supervisor said it would only be temporary. The facility decided they no longer needed security. Anyway, he said he was working on something and should call me back in a few days.

Three days passed and Sam had yet to hear back from his supervisor at the security company. Knowing this, Sheila decided to take matters into her own hands. "I'm going to work now Sam." "Okay, I'll see you later." Instead of going to work as she said, Sheila went to apply for Medicaid benefits. She had already checked to see if she would qualify and was told over the phone that it appeared that she would. She took all of the required documents and went to the office to apply. The wait was long as there seemed to be a million people. Finally, "Sheila Tucker." Shelia and the clerk went to her desk to check Sheila's information. It was determined that Sheila qualified. "Looks like you qualify Ms. Tucker. Your benefits will take about a week to process." "Thank you so much." Sheila didn't know how or even if she should tell Sam. On the one hand she knew she needed medical care as was his argument. But Sam was so proud and determined to do things his way, she couldn't possibly tell him that she had gone out and done this behind his back. However, he no longer needed to go back to doing security work in light of this. As she left the office she pondered how she would deal with this. "I'm in a real dilemma now" thought Sheila. "I can't keep it from him because he'll found out sooner or later. The problem is just how do I tell him."

Sheila went home and decided to go ahead and just tell Sam to get it over with. When she walked in the door, Sam was smiling. "Great news. My supervisor called with an assignment for me. And it's a daytime position." "Sam, I don't know how to say this but here goes. I went and applied for Medicaid and I was approved. You don't have to work security just for the benefits anymore, you can find something else now." "Why did you do that? Sam Banks doesn't take handouts I pay my own way." "I knew you'd be upset, but I thought this was the best thing to do." "You thought. You should have come to me first. I'll take care of

103

things. That's my responsibility." "Sam I told you before I'm an independent person." "I don't care Sheila. I'm going to do things how I see fit. Now I'm going to go back to work and we're going to use the benefits my job provides, is that understood!" "No, it isn't. I'm not going to give this up. What happens the next time you get laid off?" "There won't be a next time." "How can you be so sure." "Because I just know, now let's leave it at that." The two of them continued to argue until finally Sam reached for his jacket. "Why do you run out every time we can't agree on something?" asked Sheila. "Just leave me alone!" shouted Sam.

Sam walked around and stewed in anger. "How dare she go out and do something like that behind my back" he thought. "Doesn't she know me by now. She knows I don't take handouts." As he was walking, Sam came upon a bar. The last time he had drank any alcohol was the night of the accident. "I'll just go in for a minute" Sam thought. Once inside, he remembered many nights he had spent in similar surroundings. Before long he was at the bar ordering a beer. He drank that one and said to himself "that's the only one I'll get." A guy came up to him and made his acquaintance and asked if he'd like to shoot pool. Sam obliged. "Winner gets a free drink" offered the stranger. "Sure, why not" answered Sam. As the guy began to rack the balls, he thought to himself that maybe he should pass on the drink if he won. "No, I don't want to offend the guy and one more little drink won't hurt me."

Sam played pool for a couple of hours and being a pretty good player he won his fair share of games – and free drinks. By the time he got ready to leave he was pretty drunk. "You got a way home?" the stranger asked Sam. "I'm on the subway" he replied. "Can't let you ride the subway like that. Come on I'll give you a ride." "Thanks, I appreciate that."

The two of them got in the car and began to ride off. "I don't even know your name" said Sam. "James. My name is James, and you are?" "Sam, Sam Banks." "Nice to meet you Sam. Where are we off to?" Sam gave James the directions and they were on their way. About halfway into the ride, they were met with flashing blue lights. "It's the cops!" shouted James. "Just take it easy and pull over" answered Sam. "Can't do that. Got to make a run for it." With that James took off and began to lead the police on a high speed chase. "Why didn't you just pull over?" asked Sam. "This car is stolen" replied James. "Stolen!" "Yeah, hang tight." The two of them sped up the highway until they were cut off as the police had radioed ahead for assistance. "Get out of the car with your hands up!" they shouted. Sam got out of the car and said to himself "this is the worst day of my life."

Chapter 23

Feeling Forsaken

Sam was arrested and taken to the police station. He knew he was going to be in deep trouble when it was discovered he had a felony conviction for which he was currently on probation. "What kind of mess did I get myself into now?" he thought. At that moment, a guard came to the holding cell to let Sam use the phone. He didn't want to but had no choice but to call Sheila. It was about 12:30 a.m. and Sheila was a heavy sleeper. The phone rang and rang. "Please Sheila pick up the phone!" he thought. Finally, a groggy Sheila answered the phone. "Hello" she moaned. "Sheila." "Yes. Sam." "Yes baby its me. Listen, I know you're upset with me." "You've got that right." "Just hear me out. I got myself in a little trouble." "What kind of trouble Sam?" "I'm in jail." "In jail!" "Yes Sheila, calm down." "How can I calm down when you just said that you are in jail?" "Listen, I didn't do anything." "Well, why are you in jail?" "Sheila just hear me out." "No Sam. I must have gone into this too fast. I hate I trusted you and got involved with you. Goodbye!" Sheila slammed the phone down without hearing anything else Sam had to say.

The night passed and Sam awoke in a place he thought he had left behind. "I sure didn't want to come back to a place like this" he thought. Unfortunately, here he was. After breakfast he was allowed to see a public defender. He was informed that the guy he was riding with had in fact stolen the car but confessed that he acted alone and had just met Sam at the bar and was giving him a ride home. "That's great!" exclaimed Sam. "Don't get too excited" responded the lawyer. "You are a felon and this was a violation of your probation. Even though you may have been cleared of the car theft you were in his company. This won't look too good but I'll see what I can do." Sam was taken back to his cell and he thought to himself "why did this have to happen."

A week passed by and Sheila continued to refuse to accept any of Sam's calls. He had yet to get a bond hearing and didn't know exactly what he was facing. His lawyer would only give him bits and pieces of information when they spoke and Sam didn't feel very confident in his handling of the case. Then he remembered – Mr. Turner. "Mr. Turner told me to call him if I needed anything. I sure need him now." Sam gave Mr. Turner a call. "Mr. Turner." "Speaking." "This is Sam Banks, remember me." "Sam Banks, yes I remember you. How are things going for you?" "Not too good. I'm calling you from jail." "Oh no. What happened to you." Sam began to explain his situation and let Mr. Turner know that he didn't have any money. "Sam, I'm sorry I don't do pro bono work. Call me back if you can come up with some funds to retain my services. Otherwise, I suggest you get yourself a public defender." "I already have one but I don't feel good about him." "I'm sorry son, there's nothing I can do for you." Mr. Turner hung up and left Sam feeling hopeless and alone. Sheila had essentially shut him out and his longshot of getting Mr. Turner to defend him had gone up in smoke.

Another week passed by and finally Sam had his day in court. He had contacted Mr. Matthews and asked him if he would come to serve as a character witness. Since he and Tim hadn't spoken in months, Sam didn't feel as if he could call him. Sam went before the judge and pled his case. Mr. Matthews spoke highly of Sam and informed the court that until now he had experienced no problems from Sam. The judge heard all of the arguments and went to his chambers and deliberated. He returned and said these words to Sam: "Young man you must make wiser choices about the company you choose to keep. While your felony record merits punishment, the court finds that you are merely in error of bad judgment. If you are again found in violation of your probation at any time during its duration, I am recommending that it be revoked and you be required to serve the remainder of your sentence." "Thank you your honor" replied Sam. He hurriedly exited the courtroom. Just as he was about to leave Mr. Matthews called him. "Banks." "Yes Mr. Matthews." "You'd better make this the first and last time this happens." "I promise you it is."

Sam returned to the apartment to find the locks had been changed. He went to the management office to inquire about the locks and more importantly Sheila. "She moved out." "She what!" he screamed. "She moved about a couple of days ago." "You've got to be kidding, this is some kind of mistake. Sheila Tucker in 6A." "Mr. Banks, she moved out." "Did she leave a forwarding address?" "Since you're not a relative we are not required to disclose that information." "But you don't understand, she's pregnant with our child." "Mr. Banks I'm sorry but my hands are tied." Sam stormed out of the office and went to the neighbor's apartment that Sheila visited on occasion. After three knocks she opened the door. "Do you know where Sheila is?" "She asked me not to tell you." "But you've got to. She's carrying my baby." "I don't care I'm going to respect her wishes." With that she slammed the door in Sam's face.

Sam was really dejected and feeling low. Even though he was glad to be out of jail, he felt terrible because he didn't know Sheila's whereabouts. On top of that, he didn't have a place to live. To Sam it seemed as if everything and everybody in the world had turned its back on him. "Why is all of this happening to me?" he cried out. He walked to the diner to see if Sheila was there. Once he arrived he learned that she had quit two days ago. Next he went to her school to wait for her. After waiting outside of her class he saw some of her classmates but not Sheila. He asked them about her and found out that she had not been to class in almost a week. "It's as if she's dropped off the face of the earth" he thought. Sam left Sheila's school not knowing which way to go. After walking the streets aimlessly for a couple of hours he realized that he needed to find a place to sleep. With only a few dollars in his pocket, but not nearly enough to rent a motel room he went to the only place he could think of – a homeless shelter.

Chapter 24

Second Chance

Sam had seen his life go in a total tailspin from where he once was. Just a little over four years ago he was a well paid engineer on the fast track to greater things. He was financially sound and in the prime of his life. Things couldn't have been better – considering he didn't know Jesus Christ as his Lord and Savior. His life changed in one fleeting moment when he decided to drink and drive. It was a decision he had foolishly made many times before, but this time it finally caught up to him. During his rehab and incarceration he developed a relationship with God after accepting Jesus as his Lord and Savior. Even though he had to get things reestablished, he felt as if he had a new lease on life. After meeting a beautiful young lady, he lost focus of keeping God first in his life and ended up living with her and conceiving a child. Now after another momentary lapse of judgment he found himself in a stolen car which led to his being arrested again. Although he was spared further jail time, he found himself without a place to live as the woman he shared a home with turned her back on him and moved on with her life – without him.

"I can't believe this has happened to me. What did I do to deserve this?" thought Sam. Before he could wallow in his pity party he heard a bell ringing. "What's that for?" he asked the guy in the bed next to him. "That's the breakfast bell. They ring a bell for every meal. You don't answer the bell, you don't eat." Sam got in line with the others and waited for breakfast. It was similar to the prison food – only worse. "This is horrible. What have I done to myself to come to such a sad state!" The guy in front of him turned around and asked "You having troubles my man?" "Troubles, don't you realize where we are?" "Yes I do. But I thank God that I'm no longer on the streets as I once was." "You were on the street?" Sam asked. "Sure was. For three years. Until I decided to come back to God." "Come back to God?" "That's right. I had a beautiful family and a career and thought I had everything together. I didn't know the Lord or have a relationship with Him. Somebody introduced me to cocaine and the rest is history. I lost everything. Were it not for His grace and mercy I would have gone completely out of my mind and probably killed myself. But the scriptures say that *"the peace of God which passeth all understanding shall keep your hears and minds through Christ Jesus.*[51]" "Wait a second, you're a Christian?" replied Sam. "I sure am. You find that hard to believe?" "Well it's just that you're in here. I mean I accepted Christ as my Lord and Savior while I was recovering from an accident and really got to know Him while I was in prison. But you're homeless!" "What's your point? I know my situation but in spite of it I know God. I know He's able and I know He won't leave me nor will He forsake me. As I said earlier if it hadn't been for Him I would have gone completely out of my mind and who knows where I would be and if I'd even be here today." The two of them continued to talk until after breakfast was over. The guy then told Sam that he was going to a day labor pool in hopes of finding work. "You want to come?" he asked. "Why not" said Sam. "It's not like I have anything else to do."

The two of them went to the day labor pool. There were over 100 men there waiting for their shot at an assignment. After about two hours they were finally told that there were no more assignments for today. "Well, you win some and you lose some" said Sam's new friend. "How can you say that as if it doesn't matter? I need some cash, don't you?" "Look, you said you were a

Christian. Don't you know that Philippians 4:11 says '*I have learned in whatsoever state I am therewith to be content.*' Regardless of how it appears we have to trust in God and know that He is keeping us from what we truly deserve to be experiencing because of grace and mercy. When Jesus died on the cross for the sins of man He took care of everything we could possibly have need of. When He said '*It is finished*[52]' that's just what He meant. He finished the job on our behalf." Sam was taken aback by his new friend's attitude. Here they were both in a homeless shelter. While a new experience for Sam, this gentleman had been there for quite some time. Instead of complaining and moping around and being bitter, he appeared to be genuinely trusting in God and believing His Word. "This is unreal. This guy is homeless and has more faith than anyone I've ever come across" thought Sam.

Nightfall came and Sam asked the guy did he go to church. "Yes I do. There's a little church about a block from here that I attend. They've really been a blessing to me by offering me counseling, clothing and helping me out with odd jobs from time to time. Why don't you come go with me this Sunday." "I don't have anything nice to wear" was Sam's reply. "Jesus said '*Come unto me all ye that labor and are heavy laden and I will give you rest.*[53]' Now I don't see anywhere that He said what kind of clothing was required, He just said come." "Alright, I hear you. I'll go."

Sunday came and the two of them went to church. Sam hadn't been to church since he was in prison. This was the first "real church" he had been to in probably well over ten years. Even though he had just recently began to neglect his need for God and not serve Him as he once did, he felt grossly out of place. "I shouldn't have come here. I shouldn't be here" thought Sam. "Maybe I should just go back to the shelter" Sam said. "No, that's exactly what you shouldn't do. The enemy doesn't want you to hear the truth of Jesus Christ's love for you in your head and heart so he's trying to make you feel uncomfortable. James 4:7 tells us to '*resist the devil and he will flee from you.*' The devil is not going to make it easy or simple for you to come back to Christ. You've got to make the effort to overcome him through Jesus so that you can reach Jesus. Sam decided to go ahead and stay. He enjoyed hearing the choir sing, and the preacher preached a powerful sermon – yet Sam was not swayed to come back to Christ.

Sam stayed at the shelter for a few more weeks. He began to slowly integrate the things he had neglected to do back into his life. The church gave him a Bible and Sam began to read and recall scriptures that he had become familiar with. One night as he was preparing for bed, his friend got on his knees to pray. "Not that it's my business, but I don't think I've ever seen you pray." "No I don't pray" said Sam. "God doesn't want to hear what I have to say. Not after all the mistakes I've made." "You've got it all wrong. God is waiting to hear from you. The enemy deceives us into believing that we can no longer fellowship with God when we make mistakes. It's the total opposite. When we fall into sin and mistakes is when we should make every effort to draw closer to God. James 4:8 tells us to '*Draw nigh to God, and he will draw nigh to you.*' We have to make the effort to seek Him because He did all He could on the cross so He shouldn't have to and He won't force Himself upon us." "I've heard all of what you are saying before. I just don't know what I should do" replied Sam. "You must have faith."

Sam continued to go to church and read his Bible, but for some reason he just felt as if he couldn't go to God in prayer. Another Sunday came around and to Sam's surprise his favorite minister from the prison chapel, Rev. George Clark, was the guest speaker that week. "Rev. Clark." "Yes, sir." "I'm Sam Banks. You used to come to the prison I was in and preach during my incarceration. I really enjoyed you and I'm glad to see you." "It's good to see you. How are things going for you?" "Not too good. I'm homeless and living in a shelter right now." "Well I'll put you before the Lord in prayer. Remember that Psalm 121:1 tells us to '*lift up mine eyes unto the hills, from whence cometh my help.*' Never lose sight of the fact that your help comes from God and you don't have to do anything but trust Him to make provision for you. I hope that you listen and receive from the Lord on this day." "I will Rev. Clark." Rev. Clark began to preach and his sermon was a familiar story about Jesus and His forgiveness. It was the story about the woman who was taken in adultery.[54] Her accusers, ready to stone her brought her to Jesus in an attempt to trick Him regarding the situation. Jesus calmly quelled the situation by declaring to the group '*he that is without sin among you, let him first cast a stone at her.* [55]' As a result of Jesus' rebuttal, no one met the criteria and the woman was allowed to go free as Jesus gave her the command to '*go and sin no more.*[56]' Rev. Clark then made the point that man will attempt to beat you down when you falter and fail. But Jesus is right there ready to pick you up and restore you. You must remember however, just as he told this woman we must go and sin no more. This can only be accomplished by totally submitting our lives to Christ. The struggle to do so exists because our flesh is constantly coming against the spirit to do what is right in the sight of God. Unlike Jesus, man's forgiveness is conditional and subject to be withdrawn at a moment's notice. Jesus will give forgiveness that let's us know beyond a shadow of a doubt that we are loved and indeed have received true forgiveness for what it is we are guilty of. After hearing the sermon Sam, began to cry. He realized that just like the woman taken in adultery he too was being brought before Jesus. Instead of being "stoned," he could see the salvation of the Lord. Sam thought he had thrown his right to being a child of God away. But now he was aware that God could and was able to restore him. He was required to repent of his sins and not sin again just as Jesus instructed the woman.

When the time came in the service for people to accept Christ, Sam jumped up out of his seat. He went to the front of the church and embraced Rev. Clark. "Thank you. That was just what I needed to hear." "God knew that and He spoke to you today. He knows our every need Sam. We just have to trust Him to know that He can and will supply them for us." After the service was over, Sam went with some of the deacons who gave him their telephone numbers and told him they would help him to find a job and get himself back on his feet. "That's what Jesus wants us to do. He tells us in His Word '*if a man be overtaken in a fault, ye which are spiritual, restore such a one in the spirit of meekness; considering thyself, lest thou also be tempted.*[57]' Jesus is love and if we are to be like Him we are to love one another Sam." "Thank you all for your kindness. I'll definitely give you a call."

Sam went back to the shelter feeling like he did when he first accepted Christ. Only this time, Sam had a renewed resolve to see things through until the end. "I may have fallen but I intend on going all the way with Jesus as my guide." He reached the shelter and was ready to tell his friend his good news. He didn't see him anywhere around the facility so he went to ask one of the coordinators about him. Then it dawned on Sam – he had never bothered to ask the guy his name. When he described him, no one seemed to know who he was talking about. Sam remembered something God had told him earlier '*be not forgetful to entertain strangers for thereby some have entertained angels unawares.*[58]' "Could it be possible that was an angel I was dealing with?" Sam thought about it and decided that it wasn't important. The only thing that mattered was that he had renewed himself in Jesus Christ.

Chapter 25

Starting Over

Sam Banks' life had now come full circle. Even though he had lost all of the things he acquired on his own merits, the one thing he couldn't earn he held on to tightly – his salvation and victory over sin through Jesus Christ. All the things that he once thought mattered now meant virtually nothing compared to his love for Jesus. As the Apostle Paul states in Philippians 3:7-8: *'But what things were gain to me, those I counted loss for Christ. Yea doubtless, and I count all things but loss for the excellency of the knowledge of Christ Jesus my Lord for whom I have suffered the loss of all things, and do count them but dung that I may win Christ.'* The Bible tells us *'what is a man profited, if he shall gain the whole world, and lose his own soul?*[59]*'* This was a lesson Sam had come to learn for himself. In spite of all the trappings of this world, he was miserable without Jesus Christ. Money, fame, prestige and fortune can't compensate to the peace and security of resting in Jesus Christ and His good and perfect will for your life. Sam now truly recognized this and was ready to embark anew on his journey with Christ Jesus.

"I may have lost everything I thought was important to me but as long as I have Jesus Christ, I have all that I need in and through Him" said Sam. He continued to live at the shelter and work odd jobs at the church. Just as promised the deacons helped him to find a part time job that eventually became a full time position. Sam began to slowly rebuild the pieces to his life. This time however, he went about it in a totally different manner – with Jesus leading the way. Before long he was able to get an apartment and things were beginning to take off.

One night after a long day at work, a tired Sam plopped down on his couch and reflected on the past five years of his life. He looked at how he had been spared from doing even more time than he deserved and was required as a result of the plea bargain. Next he noticed that God sent what it was he needed for that particular time in his life. When he got jailed the first time, God introduced Phil to his life. Just as he and Phil got to know one another he took Phil away. Once in prison, he met Stan and was able to share Jesus Christ with him and get the joy of knowing that Stan accepted Jesus as his Lord and Savior before his death. He was also able to minister to Jeff as God used him to break down the walls Jeff had built up to keep Him out of his life. While he was at the shelter, he met a man that helped lead him back to Christ. Reflecting on all these things, Sam began to pray: "God, I thank you for allowing me the opportunity to start fresh with a clean slate. I appreciate all that you've done for me and I know that even though I didn't deserve it your grace and mercy saw fit to give me another chance." At that moment, God began to speak to Sam. "Sam." "Yes God." "Sam I finally have your attention again. I stand at the door and knock. I can't nor will I force my way into your life. *I will never leave thee, nor forsake thee.*[60] Sam you must recognize that it was never me that abandoned you. I promised you that would never happen. Even when you were operating on your own terms I was right there observing you and making sure that you didn't get too far away from me. *I the Lord am your keeper.*[61] Remember that I don't want you to stray away from me. I sent for you as would a shepherd a lost sheep.[62] It is not my desire that you should perish. My will for your life is that *you would have life and that you would have it more abundantly.*[63] Man will pressure you into thinking you need to have material possessions to be esteemed greatly. But my desire is that you *seek first the kingdom of God and his right-eousness and all these things shall be added unto you.*[64] It takes faith to believe and trust in Me because the manner in which I operate greatly differs from the ways of man. As a result man has trouble following Me because he can't control My every move. But you must know this Sam, My Word declares that '*no good thing will he withhold from them that walk uprightly.*[65]' Continue to walk after My ways and stay safely in My will for your life."

"Thank you God for loving me and for keeping me."

Sam continued to remain steadfast in the Word of God and he was faithful and diligent in his service to the Lord at the church. The church began to grow and an influx of young families began to move into the community. Upon seeing this, the pastor decided to start a day care center/school. In about a year's time they had made preparations to begin laying the foundation for their project. Sam was heavily involved as he desperately wanted a second shot at teaching. "What better way to serve God and help my fellow man than to teach and be an example to young people" he thought.

After much prayer and planning, the time had finally come for the school to open its doors. Many parents in the community supported the idea. The neighborhood children comprised about 70% of the school's enrollment and things were looking great. Sam had petitioned hard for a teaching position at the school and the pastor decided to give him a shot. He started out teaching math to students at the 4th and 5th grade levels.

Sam was really enjoying his opportunity to serve God through this capacity. "God I thank you for using me and allowing me this second chance to serve you." About halfway through the semester, one of his students was having problems in his studies. Noticing this, Sam began to help the youngster through after school tutoring sessions. As a result of this, he started a tutorial program for students not only at the school but in the community at large.

The end of the school year arrived and Sam looked back at the year with great pride. The school had gotten off to an excellent start and was a big success not only for the church's welfare but the community as well. Sam had played a very significant role in helping things to run smoothly and get off the ground and running. He was instrumental in not only starting the tutorial sessions but also a mentoring program. For his efforts, Sam was honored as the teacher of the year at the school's first annual awards banquet. Upon reflecting on all that he had been through to arrive at this moment Sam was quick to acknowledge the God was the reason for all that had happened and he was merely the instrument used to accomplish His will. He was able to recognize that through Jesus Christ he was more than an overcomer as the Word of God declares His children to be. Sam Banks was a living testimony of what God's unconditional, agape love can and will do in our lives if we allow it. What started out as a struggle, turned out to be a triumph for the glory of God!

Epilogue

Sam Banks, although a fictional character, is someone that all Christians, male or female, can relate to as we walk along our respective Christian journeys. There are times we are riding high in Christ and times when we feel low in the valley all alone. We must remember to always keep our heads lifted up and looking up as the Word of God compels us to. Secondly, as Christians we must be ever mindful not to allow ourselves to be found guilty of compromise. There is NEVER a situation that will provide excuse or appropriate reason for us to do so. Thanks to Jesus Christ, we are victorious over sin through Him and know that we are MORE than conquerors! As such, we should always walk in a posture of victory and authority rather than defeated and powerless.

Looking at Sam Banks, one could quite possibly parallel their life with circumstances and events that he experienced and went through. We must recognize that in spite of what we attempt or seek to do, God's will is perfect and unfailing. As such, it will go forth regardless of what we do to circumvent or sidestep what He has decided is best for us. Also, we must know that the things we go after and attain on our own merits without God's blessing/approval, will surely be taken away and be of no benefit to us unlike what God has in His storehouse at the ready to provide for our well being and most importantly His glory.

It is my prayer that THE STRUGGLE will be a blessing to your Christian walk and that even the non-believer may come to know Christ for the free pardon of his/her sins and see this as a message from God Himself that even though we struggle at times, just like Sam Banks, you too can have victory in your life. May God bless you and thank you for supporting His gift by reading this work that He gave me to share with His people.

References

[1] John 20:29 (partial reference)
[2] Proverbs 3:5-6 (partial references).
[3] Numbers 23:19 (partial reference)
[4] Hebrews 11:6 (partial reference).
[5] Hebrews 11:6 (partial reference).
[6] Genesis 1:1
[7] Romans 12:3 (partial reference).
[8] Galatians 6:7 (partial reference).
[9] Revelation 3:20 (partial reference).
[10] Philippians 4:13
[11] Matthew 7:7
[12] Psalm 121:5 (partial reference).
[13] Romans 5:6
[14] Hebrews 11:6 (partial reference).
[15] Romans 3:23.
[16] Romans 14:23 (partial reference).
[17] Psalm 23:1.
[18] Romans 2:11.
[19] Proverbs 3:5-6 (partial references).
[20] John 15:16.
[21] John 15:16 (partial reference).
[22] Romans 8:28 (partial reference).
[23] Romans 2:11.
[24] 1 Corinthians 3:7.
[25] Ephesians 4:26 (partial reference).
[26] Job 38:3; 40:2, 7, 9 (partial references).
[27] Matthew 5:16.
[28] Psalm 119:105.
[29] Matthew 6:24 (partial reference).
[30] Philippians 4:6.
[31] Matthew 10:19 (partial reference).
[32] Matthew 4:4.
[33] 2 Timothy 2:15.
[34] Hebrews 11:6.
[35] Matthew 24:36.
[36] Hebrews 10:25.
[37] James 4:4 (partial reference).
[38] Psalm 53:1 (partial reference).
[39] Matthew 11:29-30.

[40] 2 Corinthians 3:17 (partial reference).

[41] Philippians 2:5.

[42] Hebrews 13:2.

[43] Matthew 28:20 (partial reference).

[44] Psalm 84:11 (partial reference).

[45] James 1:17 (partial reference).

[46] Luke 18:27.

[47] Philippians 4:19.

[48] Philippians 4:7 (partial reference).

[49] Revelation 3:20.

[50] Hebrews 11:6 (partial reference).

[51] Philippians 4:7.

[52] John 19:30 (partial reference).

[53] Matthew 11:28.

[54] John 8:3-11.

[55] John 8:7 (partial reference).

[56] John 8:11 (partial reference).

[57] Galatians 6:1.

[58] Hebrews 13:2.

[59] Matthew 16:26 (partial reference).

[60] Hebrews 13:5 (partial reference).

[61] Psalm 121:5 (partial reference).

[62] Matthew 18:10-14.

[63] John 10:10 (partial reference).

[64] Matthew 6:33.

[65] Psalm 84:11 (partial reference).